SHANGHAI
PRINCESS

SHANGHAI
PRINCESS

HER SURVIVAL WITH PRIDE & DIGNITY

By Chen Danyan

Better Link Press

This book is edited and designed by the Editorial Committee of *Cultural China* series

Managing Directors: Wang Youbu, Xu Naiqing
Editorial Director: Wu Ying
Editors: Daniel Clutton, Yang Xinci

Text by Chen Danyan
Translation by Mavis Gock Yen
Images provided by Woo Zhongzheng

Interior and Cover Design by Wang Wei

ISBN: 978-1-60220-218-4

Address any comments about *Shanghai Princess: Her Survival with Pride &
Dignity* to:

Better Link Press
99 Park Ave
New York, NY 10016
USA

or

Shanghai Press and Publishing Development Company
F 7 Donghu Road, Shanghai, China (200031)
Email: comments_betterlinkpress@hotmail.com

Printed in China by Shenzhen Donnelley Printing Co. Ltd.

1 2 3 4 5 6 7 8 9 10

Contents

Transliteration

In the main, names and terms are given as they were familiarly known at the time of the events described. They include early place names adopted by the Chinese Post Office; the Wade-Giles system, spellings based on the dialect spoken in Peking; variations adopted by business circles in Shanghai; and the system used in Hong Kong based on Cantonese pronunciation and of particular relevance to the Chinese in Australia. Otherwise the Pinyin system, officially adopted by China in the 1970s, is used.

Chapter One

1910
One Year Old
Sydney

A Pair of White Bootees

There were 2 gardens. The first was what we called the Rose Garden. Dadda loved flowers, especially roses, so the flower beds were full of different varieties. At the end of this garden was a trellis, which was covered with a climbing variety of roses. Beyond the trellis was the second garden. It had a lawn in the middle with flower beds surrounding it.

Daisy Kwok faces the camera serenely on her first birthday, 2 April 1910, in Sydney, Australia.

Chapter 1 A Pair of White Bootees

*I*t was the second of April, 1910. Perhaps those tall Australian trees had already shed many leaves in the sunshine and wind. Had the chrysanthemums already dropped their buds as in the old English song about roses? It was one of countless Australian autumns. But I have no way of knowing.

Nor was the little girl in the photograph able to recall this. On the 24th of September, 1998, she took another look at the photo, stretching out her hand to touch this first birthday image of herself, exclaiming:

"Is this my daughter? I can't believe this is my first birthday photo."

She touched the little girl's porcelain-like forehead with a life-wrinkled finger.

Was the photographer's floor a wooden one? Did the white lacy dress rustle? Were slides used? Did it take long? Was it easy for the little girl to pose so peacefully and seriously? No one knows now. Her father drove her and her mother to the photographer's but he died in Shanghai in 1932 when she was already an attractive girl not yet graduated from Yenching University. When her mother died in Shanghai in 1947, she was a beautiful young matron with two children of her own. But the memories of these events in Sydney's Campbell Street disappeared forever with the passing of her parents.

I was born in Campbell Street, Sydney, on April 2, 1909. I was the seventh child. Later on we moved to Dowling Street, a house opposite a public park. All I remember of the house is that I had diphtheria there, and passed it on to Edie and Percy. I think I was kept isolated on the porch. When I was about 4 or 5, we moved to 2 Croydon Street, Petersham. Dadda had bought this house. There were 2 gardens, a large chicken coop, a pigeon house, stables for our two ponies and a yard with a well in it. The well was no longer in use of course.

She wore a lacy white dress. She was the seventh child and her well-to-do parents wanted her to have a first birthday photograph as a reminder of her start in life. Did they wish her a life of one hundred years? Plump and serene, her soft-soled shoes facing the camera had not a speck of dust on them. She could hardly walk then, so nothing could soil her shoes. Perhaps her father said:

"Smile, Daisy dear."

Coming from his home in Zhongshan County and building his prosperity in the fruit trade, he loved this seventh child most of all. He had her crib placed next to his own bedroom so he could attend to her at night. More about these happenings in 1910 I have no way of knowing, but Daisy left detailed descriptions of their old home in the draft of her memoirs.

THE HOUSE WE LIVED IN (2 Croydon St., Petersham, Sydney)

I had a letter from my brother, Georgie(nickname of George), in Honolulu telling me he had a picture of our old family homestead in Australia. I asked him to send it to me as the news brought back so many memories. Georgie had just taken a trip to Sydney and had visited the old house, which was still there. I was 8 years old when we left Australia, but I still had a vivid memory of the house.

The main entrance was a gate, which led to the steps to the front door. However, I usually entered the house by turning to the right and going into the garden and then around to a back entrance. There were 2 gardens, the first was what we called the Rose Garden. Dadda loved flowers, especially roses, so the flower beds were full of different varieties. At the end of this garden was a trellis, which was covered with a climbing variety of roses. Beyond the trellis was the second garden. It had a lawn in the middle with flower beds surrounding it.

Beside this garden was what we called the "well yard," as there was a well, of course no longer with any water in it. From this garden I could enter the house up some steps, which led to an enclosed porch. Beyond the well yard were the stables. We had 2 ponies. A gate in this yard was the back entrance through which the sulky and phaeton could go.

It was an old fashioned 2-storied house. When we moved in, the gas jets were still there, but we used electricity.

The front door opened into a long hallway. On the left was the living room or parlor, a very large room. I remember that it was big enough to hold two sets of furniture. On the other side of the hall were 2 rooms. The first was called the study, but actually in it was a long table on which Dad kept albums of his old cronies. When they came to visit, they would go over the pictures to recall their earlier days together. We youngsters were not very interested in these albums, but to Dadda they were his prize possessions and he even took them back to China with us.

These three rooms were rarely used except for entertaining, especially for the Sunday lunches which I described elsewhere. Breakfast and lunch were eaten in the kitchen, but dinner was served in the dining room. As a rule we ate western style food, as our maid was an Australian. Next to the kitchen was the laundry. A side entrance was in the kitchen. This opened onto a lane which led to the front of the house(Croydon St.) That completes the ground floor.

The stairway at the end of the hall led to two more hallways, one lower than the other. The larger on the right led towards the front of the house where there were 5 bedrooms. The first two, which overlooked the street, were my father's and mother's rooms. Next to Dad's room on the right side of the hall was Leon and Wally's room. Opposite them were 2 smaller rooms, one for Edie and the other for Pearlie and Elsie. I slept in Dadda's room and Georgie in Mum's.

The other hallway led past two rooms to the bathroom and toilet. Percy occupied the first room while the other was for the maid.

I might add here that Dad's and Mum's rooms opened onto a long veranda overlooking Croydon St. That is the house as I remember it.

This description contrasts sharply with the outbreak of the Cultural Revolution in 1966 when Daisy and her son, Zhongzheng, were driven out of their home to live in an attic. The roof of the attic leaked. They were forced out of their home in winter in the madness of the initial period of the Cultural Revolution. Daisy's recollections of that period are incomplete and fragmentary, but I could well imagine the pain she went through just thinking about it. The way she switched from writing about the happenings in 1966 to recall her childhood home in 1910, suggests that old house was the best and safest place she had known in her life.

Who could have foretold in 1910 what threats this world would bring to her?

Everyone saw her as blessed with good fortune. Nothing but a bright future awaited this healthy and beautiful child. Who could have imagined that in 1972 after she retired she would live alone in a tiny north-facing attic, all her possessions long lost or confiscated, that she would have to depend on a monthly pension of thirty-six yuan, sufficient only in 1972 to buy the simplest of food. In winter, even the air she breathed out would quickly freeze, while in the summer, she would sit on her doorstep hoping a breeze might blow her way from the south.

On the evening of the 25th of September 1998, she peacefully passed away in her own home. The Shanghai Red Cross Society and the Shanghai Medical University took away her body. In 1985 she had of her own free will decided to donate her remains to the Red Cross Society. By then her son's family had already moved to the United States, while her second husband, David Wang, had died two years earlier when she was seventy-four. Thus in the autumn of 1998, her ninety-year old body made its last trip through the streets of Shanghai in a Red Cross Society vehicle.

Daisy first arrived in Shanghai in 1918 with the rest of her family. Before leaving she innocently told her playmates:

"Dad is taking the whole family to a restaurant called Shanghai."

Shanghai was neither Daisy's birthplace, nor her native home. By 1949 most of her brothers and sisters had left together with their families. But Daisy remained. In 1969 she was sent to Chongming Island to be remolded through labor and was dubbed by others there as "that old foreign woman." Only in 1990 did she finally pay a return visit to her birthplace of Australia, after which she returned to Shanghai. She later went to the United States but again she returned to Shanghai. The donation of her remains to medical research was her final gift to Shanghai. The Australian Consul-General in Shanghai, as the representative of Daisy's native home, also paid his last respects at her memorial service. Actually, Daisy's funeral took place in the dissecting room of the medical institute.

Lying beneath the shadowless lamp, her fringe cut short, her forehead looked as it had when she was one year old. Her serenity was clear, glistening like a pebble after ninety years of water had passed over it. A ceiling of glass surrounded the shadowless lights. I wondered if, as the medical students stood there and watched their instructors, they noticed the expression on her face.

Mozart's *Requiem* was played at the memorial service and Daisy was dressed in her favorite Chinese-style black jacket. For 60 years she had given up wearing western clothes. She looked upon herself as Chinese and believed she should wear Chinese-style clothes, just as she had in the twenties and thirties, the height of her halcyon days. Officials from the Overseas Chinese Office said they had only just learned she was a Chinese from overseas, who returned to China as a child. She had never mentioned this to them before.

The small icy room's wall of green tiles was covered with 36 arrangements of fresh flowers, their scent redolent of their fleeting life. There were many white lilies, their pure white color and splendor matching that of Daisy. There were also many unopened chrysanthemum buds, because she always liked chrysanthemums. Her English name was Daisy, meaning chrysanthemum; they shared the same name. Fresh flowers surrounded her and her photograph.

I called on her on the afternoon of September 24th with some white roses, which she placed in water on top of the small green cupboard. This was one of the very few articles of furniture she was allowed to take with her when she was driven from her home in 1966. As she re-arranged the roses, she said:

"You know how I love flowers. They are so beautiful."

She too looked beautiful that day. Her snow-white hair had been freshly permed. Those were her twilight days. I wonder if thoughts of the garden in her old home in Australia crossed her mind that day, the roses her Dad had planted. She loved fresh flowers, just like her father.

In her last days she said she sometimes saw reflections floating against the ceiling, but she knew they were spirits, she was not afraid. Perhaps they were the spirits of her dear ones, come to receive her, just as when she was one -year-old she was driven to the photographer's and now they had come to take her to their place of reunion.

Chapter Two

1915
Six Years Old

A Chinese Restaurant called "Shanghai"

Daisy used to watch her Dad taking her Mum and elder sister to the opera. They would dress up on such occasions and there was always a box of chocolates. As a result she grew up looking forward to a similar future.

*I*n September 1987 she left Shanghai to visit her son, Zhongzheng, and his family in the United States, as well as other members of her own family whom she had not seen for more than 30 years.

Her husband, Woo Yu-hsiang, had been arrested in 1958 and ordered to repay the government US$64,000. At the time Daisy had written to her relatives abroad asking for financial help. Of all the many letters she wrote however, only Wally responded. He sent her US$8,000, a loan she had earlier made to him. When she started teaching English in 1962, he also sent her English textbooks and the latest edition of a dictionary. But she lost contact with him after the Cultural Revolution began.

As children, Wally had always been the leader of the two, making all sorts of suggestions to her. During their 6-week sea-trip to Shanghai on a Japanese mail boat, their favorite game had been "follow the leader." This was when his leadership over her became firmly established.

Before the family left Sydney their parents took them to the photographer's. Daisy was then taller than Wally but he insisted she be seated so that he would appear to be the taller. They were the closest among all their siblings. While Daisy was in her teens, Wally suggested she should learn to play the piano as well as drive a car, then considered fashionable pursuits for girls belonging to Shanghai's social elite.

In 1956 Daisy's youngest brother, George, suddenly departed for Guangzhou, from where he slipped across the border into Hong Kong. While clearing out his desk before leaving, he discovered a secret drawer containing a revolver belonging to his second elder brother, Leon. In 1947 T. V. Soong had helped the Wing On Company overcome a financial crisis. As a result Leon had been appointed the company's director. However, earlier in 1948, the capitalists in Shanghai were pressed to surrender their foreign exchange holdings in order to bolster the issue of a new currency by the Nanjing Government. This drive was conducted by Chiang Ching-kuo, a son of Chiang Kai-shek. Fearing for his personal safety Leon handed over his desk to his younger brother George and fled overseas. George was only one of the managers. The night before George left for Guangzhou in 1956, he took the revolver to Daisy and asked her to get rid of it. It was possession of this firearm, which had never been used that became one of the crimes listed against Daisy's husband, Woo Yu-hsiang, who buried the revolver beneath a tree in their garden.

The younger Kwok Bew children with the eldest daughter, Edie, before they left Sydney for Shanghai in 1917, taking with them the free and easy outlook of the people of Oceania.

George never knew what happened after he left Shanghai. When Daisy met him again he and his wife were running a beauty parlor in Hawaii. He was wearing shirts splashed with floral designs, a popular Hawaiian fashion. With age he looked more like an older man of Jewish background, rather than the pudgy little boy in the early family photo. Daisy never really told George about the outcome of the revolver. She felt there was no point in doing so.

Daisy's third sister, Elsie, had been chosen as the first Miss Shanghai. The early family photos had shown her promising to develop into an attractive and lively young woman. By the time of Daisy's visit she and her husband had passed away after spending years in the United States. After she and her sisters had graduated from McTyeire School for Girls, Elsie had become an accomplished horsewoman, dancer, and markswoman. McTyeire School for Girls was founded in 1890 by the Southern Methodist Mission to train the daughters of Shanghai's elite families for their future role as society hostesses. Instruction was in English and most of the teachers were Westerners. Once Elsie took Daisy out to race with other cars and it turned out that one car they were trying to overtake was driven by Wally. Elsie entered the Miss Shanghai competition after Daisy had gone to Peking to study psychology. Daisy then wrote to Elsie urging her to give up her senseless activities. But when Elsie wanted to elope with the man she loved, Daisy was the first to support her. Elsie died in the United States in 1980 and Daisy went there too late to see her again. She was only able to meet her eldest sister Edie, who was standing affectionately at the back of the younger siblings in the photo.

Upon her arrival in the United States, Daisy was urged to write the story of her life. She therefore spent a whole summer doing two university writing courses with a view to brush up her English writing skill. From the time she had left Australia in her childhood she had always attended English-speaking schools and had mostly spoken and used English. Gradually she became more familiar with Chinese after entering middle school, but never as her native tongue. It was not until the fifties when members of the old capitalist class were compelled to undergo brain-washing that she took up the study of Chinese seriously. Finally in 1971 the time came for the members of the old capitalist class Daisy was working with to retire. They were given a final dressing down by the rebel red guards in charge of them and called on to tell how they intended to continue their ideological remolding. When Daisy said she would continue to study Chinese in order to be able to go on studying Mao's works, she was praised.

She started to write her memoirs in September 1989.

I attended the primary school on Crystal Street, just around the corner from where we lived. I started from kindergarten. On Sundays we went to Sunday school. Our parents attended the Cantonese church down town. Dadda gave each of us (Elsie, Wally and me) a penny for the collection box. One day on our way to Sunday school Wally said he would show us another route. He stopped at an ice-cream parlor and suggested we have an ice cream cone. He told me to use the penny to buy the cone and use the half-penny change for the collection plate. That was Wally! However, I always did what he told me to do.

There was much racial discrimination in both schools. The children at Sunday School called me all sorts of names, so I decided not to go there again. One day the headmaster came to find out what was wrong. My mother answered the door bell. I followed her to the door, and when I saw who it was I hid behind her. When I heard his complaint I stepped forward and told him I was not going to attend Sunday School as long as I was being called names.

Her memoirs also revealed how deeply impressed she was by her parents' and elder sister's visits to the opera.

"How I longed to grow up and go with them," she wrote.

In 1917 her father, George Kwok Bew[1], in response to Dr. Sun Yat-sen's invitation, arrived in Shanghai with a fellow clansman, Kwok Gew. Shanghai was where the modern department store of the Wing On Company was being established. Daisy's mother and the younger children followed later. They stayed in the Oriental Hotel, owned by her mother's Ma clan. The Mas had already set up the Sincere Department Store opposite the site of the Wing On Company. Daisy would look out of the hotel window at the rising layers of the Wing On building, still covered with green bamboo scaffolding. In those early days the appearance of these new department stores symbolized the growth of Chinese capital and the economic development that was taking place in Shanghai.

One day Daisy noticed something white floating outside the hotel window. She opened the window and stretched out her hand to catch some of the white material and then rushed to her mother's room. By this time only a few drops of water remained in her hand. Her mother laughed and explained that this was snow, which Daisy had never seen before in Sydney.

Our Uncle Gock Lock, whose first wife was my mother's sister, also lived in the same hotel. He was to be the managing director of the new Wing On Company with my father. He had a Ford car, which was considered very luxurious in those days. Sometimes he took us out to the countryside. Actually we only went as far as the Bubbling Well but at that time it was open space. We felt we had driven a long, long way.

Unconsciously, Daisy's memoirs reflect a child's sense of peaceful security. In fact, no one knew what lay ahead of them. Daisy had no idea that in 1967 she and fellow teachers from her school, considered to have "problems", such as a capitalist background, would be sent to a factory to work. One day over lunch, they spoke to each other in English. Asked what she intended to do during the break, Daisy said she wanted to go to the Park Hotel to buy some bread. Then she added, "You know, the bread they make now is better than before Liberation (1949)."

I think she must have said this deliberately because she noticed two of the factory workers sitting at the same table as them. After the break these teachers were unexpectedly told to wait in a small downstairs room. At first they thought there was going to be a meeting from which the capitalist elements would be excluded. But as they went below, they realized a whole roomful of people were waiting for them.

The worker-in-charge asked all those who knew English to stand up in front and Daisy did so. She noticed that one of the workers who had shared a table with them at lunch was also present. He fetched the two other teachers who were at the same table to the front.

He came forward and told me to kneel down. I did. He tapped me on the head. Out of curiosity I looked up to see what he had hit me with. It was a broom. I wondered whether they meant to beat me up, but instead he told me to report what I had said while working upstairs. I told them in Chinese. He accused me of lying. "I understand English," he said, "didn't you mention the word 'park'? You intended going to the park at lunch time. Who were you going to meet there? And for what?" I told him I was going to the Park Hotel, not the park. "Oh yes," he said, "you claimed that the bread after Liberation was no good. Do you deny that you had mentioned the park and bread?"

That shows how things could be twisted. After a few more taps on the head with the broom the meeting was adjourned. He felt he had exposed how bad and dishonest a capitalist was.

How could Daisy have known back in 1915 that one day she would have to confront such humiliation! Yet she was able to live on in the face of it without becoming broken-hearted or an embittered old person.

[1]**George Kwok Bew:** was a proprietor of the Wing Sang Company, one of the biggest banana agents in Sydney. He played a leading part in the extension of support to Dr. Sun Yat-sen's republican cause by the Chinese in Australia in the early 1900s. The rise of the Chinese merchant elite was made possible by the flourishing banana growing industry in northern Queensland in the 1880s and 1890s. They also developed a fruit trade with Fiji. The origin of the three biggest department stores, the Wing On, the Sincere and the Sun, in Hong Kong, Guangzhou and Shanghai could be traced to the fruit companies in Sydney and Melbourne. The earliest, the Sincere & Company Ltd in Hong Kong, was founded in 1900. It grew out of the Wing Sang & Company, set up in 1890. The largest, the Wing On & Company, was opened in Hong Kong in 1907, having as its origin a Sydney Chinese fruit store set up in 1897.

Overseas Chinese played a significant part in fostering Chinese nationalism. After 1911 George Kwok Bew and a few other merchants supported Sun Yat-sen. They provided the support and funds needed to win a sweeping victory. The Chinese community, particularly those from Zhongshan County, looked upon George Kwok Bew as their leader and friend. Kwok Bew was a proprietor of the Wing Sang Company. But the Kwoks, Mas and Lis lived in neighboring villages. They intermarried.

When he returned to China in 1917 his fellow clansmen in the Wing On Company finally succeeded in persuading him to enhance the Wing On Company's biggest department store in Shanghai with his name by becoming its first director. He was also appointed head of the Central Mint set up by Dr. Sun Yat-sen. His signature appeared on all the banknotes.

See: Yong, C. F., *The New Golden Mountain*, (Raphael Arts Pty. 1977)

Yong, C.F., "The Banana Trade and the Chinese in New South Wales and Victoria", ANU Historical Journal, 1965-66 V.1. No. 2 pp. 28-35.

Yong, C.F., "The Chinese Revolution of 1911: Reactions of Chinese in New South Wales and Victoria", Historical Studies, Australia and New Zealand, V. 2, No. 46, April 1966, pp. 213-229.

Chapter Three

1920
Eleven Years Old

Schooldays in Shanghai

Sometimes one wonders if a person's character is formed in childhood, surely a rich and happy life would best nourish purity and tenacity.

Front entrance to McTyeire School for Girls in Shanghai.

*A*n old torn photo shows the sun shining on the grounds of the Mc-Tyeire Girls' School , the only way of knowing what the weather was like that day. In fact the light shone afresh each day, just like the water in a river, never to return.

By the 1920s McTyeire had moved from its premises at the Moore Memorial Church in Xizang Road to the Ching Family garden. Founded by American Protestant missionaries, the school was already 28 years old. From the very first day of its establishment, it had the support of the Shanghai regional Tao Tai, Nieh Zhong-fang, and was acclaimed as one of Shanghai's new-type schools. Its purpose was to prepare the daughters of Shanghai's elite families for their future role in life. By the time of Daisy's admission, the national mother of China, Soong Ching Ling, and the first lady of the land, Soong Mei-ling, had already graduated.

The fees charged at McTyeire were extraordinarily high. A strict discipline was imposed on the students. Within the dormitories, the 6 x 4.5 feet wide beds were covered in white sheets. Every student was required to make her own bed. Not the slightest negligence was permitted. While at the school the students had to divest themselves of all expensive jewelry, under threat of confiscation. They also had to follow a rigid code of conduct. For example, when pausing in a corridor to speak to someone else, they had to step to one side. Family origin was no excuse for any divergence.

The aim of the school was to cultivate a love of people and of life. The curriculum was American, with the emphasis on physical training, English, music and science. The dramatic performances put on by the school were considered to be outstanding. American textbooks were used and the students were taught that China lay in the Far East. The library contained all the American and British literary classics, as well as the latest English magazines and contemporary American popular literature such as *Pollyanna*. Also available was the English language edition of Karl Marx's *Capital*.

The style of the school was aristocratic. The students were being prepared to become society hostesses. Breakfast included such Chinese luxuries as desiccated meat and western-style butter. The students' sitting room was furnished with sofas, carpets and a phonograph. They were encouraged to develop strong characters, to be refined as well as persevering. Character development was based on a youthful spirit and optimism.

In those days it was a popular trend for Shanghai's elite to have a holiday retreat in the western suburbs, an American motor car, a drawer full of neckties for the husband and a daughter attending McTyeire School for Girls. Even middle-class families were economizing on housing, food and clothing, in order to send their daughters to

Daisy play-acting in the 1920s,
still a plump young girl.

McTyeire. Ambitious families wanted their daughters to receive the best American-style education available. Just as McTyeire claimed, they believed the type of education it provided would instill in their daughters the need for brave hearts and exemplary behaviour, the best possible foundation for life. As for the unambitious, they believed the school would broaden the horizons of their daughters by enhancing their status with its name as well as western modernization, leading to marriage into desirable families. They looked upon graduation from McTyeire as a valuable part of a young girl's dowry.

Daisy's photos showed that she settled in well at McTyeire. She took part in the school's dramatic society and performed in Shakespeare's *Taming of the Shrew*. She was uncertain whether one of the photos was taken before or after a performance, but it shows her sitting with a fellow student playing the role of a member of the gentry. Daisy looks a happy young girl, with a bandanna round her head, coyly enjoying being sought after by her companion. But closer inspection reveals a child-like pleasure in play acting! Supposedly playing the role of a young girl in love, the photo is more suggestive of a little girl playing mother with her dolls. In another photo of a just- married couple, the stance of the girl playing the groom, also a member of the gentry, was no doubt copied from her father. There is no sign at all of how a young man might feel on his wedding day, pleasure at winning the hand of a beautiful girl, fear of responsibility, regret over the loss of his bachelorhood, worry about how they would manage. Living in a world of girls, she naturally knew very little about young men. As for Daisy in the role of the bride, she appears totally muddled. Also imitating others, her arm is linked with the groom as she stands upright, wearing a long stage bridal veil. She too knows nothing about marriage, but she shows no fear. Unlike other young girls, she neither fawns nor reveals amorous feelings. Perhaps facing the unknown bravely was an endowment from her schooling at McTyeire.

The students probably collapsed in fits of laughter after being photographed, as is common with young girls. There is no doubt, however, that these were the happiest days of Daisy's life.

Daisy left the first Cantonese school she attended, finding it unsuitable. From the time she was a small girl she had always been able to extricate herself from a disagreeable situation. In 1918 when she was sent to the Cantonese school she could not speak a word of Cantonese, nor could she speak the Shanghai dialect. The teacher gave her a Chinese name but on the way home in a rickshaw the piece of paper on which her new name was written was blown away and she could not remember it. She and her siblings used to buy their lunch outside instead of returning home. But the only word they knew was *mian* for noodles, so every school day they ate noodles. Neither could Daisy use chopsticks. No matter how hard she tried she could not manipulate them properly. So one misty Shanghai weekend, the family moved her and her siblings to missionary schools, away from chopsticks and the teachers, who always called on Kwok to stand up and answer questions in Cantonese.

Daisy finally made friends with a girl in high school who gave her the same name as the then popular writer Hsieh Wen-ying. Only after that could Daisy be said to have a proper Chinese name. Much later on, Daisy met the famous writer, Hsieh Ping-hsin, in Peking, and she remarked:

"But we have the same name!"

Daisy then explained how it had all come about.

This was the way Daisy lightheartedly pursued her objectives. Nobody ever imagined that one day Daisy would have to stand in the marketplace selling salted duck eggs, that she would only be able to afford a bowl of plain noodles for her supper, would have to travel from the farm where she was being reformed through labor to hear the court sentence handed down on her husband, followed by the total confiscation of her properties. Not even her wedding dress was excluded. Nonetheless, she survived. Years afterwards when an overseas visitor asked her about the time she spent being reformed through labor, she sat up sprightly and said:

"But that helped me to keep slim!"

"When Daisy was 86, three young girls took her out to dinner. After only a few minutes in her company they felt that this was no old lady, while they themselves were more like young admirers vying to entertain a staggeringly beautiful woman.

This is why I wonder about the purity and tenacity of a person's character! Surely such qualities are best cultivated in a rich and cultured childhood rather than in a bitter and poverty-stricken life!

After Daisy transferred to McTyeire her minuses became the pluses so eagerly sought after by her fellow students. At McTyeire they were required to speak, read and write in English. The exams and all classes were given in English. By 1919 she had entered the 5th grade with all A's. She was a happy child, lacking for nothing.

Comparison is inevitable wherever there are more girls and Daisy came out on top. Although she had not yet reached the striking age of 20 there was already no doubt about her beauty. When the girls from well-to-do families compared their backgrounds, she came out first. Attending a foreign school, naturally they compared each other's command of English and here she was first too. She was totally unaffected by any discrimination.

Meanwhile, the Wing On Company was gaining in prestige daily. Its roof garden had become the most fashionable place along Nanjing Road. Her family had moved to a western-style house with a beautiful garden, bought from a Swede. Her room was next to her Dad's

Daisy and friends at McTyeire. In her nineties, Chiang Yen-wen (b. centre) who shared 70 years of friendship with Daisy, was still living in Peking, where she was envied by young girls for her fine features. She said Daisy was really a perfectionist from the time she was small. During their middle and high school days, Daisy chose to sacrifice her weekend leave rather than give a piano performance at her teacher's request, believing her mastery of the piano was not good enough. Perhaps this explains the development of her stubborn determination in later life.

bedroom and she was still her father's favorite child. At home she continued to work in the garden with her father, as they both liked cultivating flowers.

Her father's company was already regarded as the largest of its kind. Also he had been appointed head of the central mint, founded by Dr. Sun Yat-sen. Daisy's father had a sack full of dud copper coins. When the Kwok children played in the garden they would take a handful of coins to throw into the pond to make bubbles.

Daisy learned from her father the value of string. Although he made his way up in the world through fruit marketing, he always wound little pieces of string into balls and placed them in a drawer for future use, even after his children had grown up, were riding in bullet-proof cars and had bodyguards. Daisy acquired this habit from her father. After her death, her children found a drawer full of balls of string in her home.

Due to the danger of kidnapping, the Kwok children seldom went out socially. Their best friends were mostly from the Soong family. T. V. Soong used to have dinner in the Kwok household every day. His sister, Soong Mei-ling, took care of the accounts in the Soong household while Pearlie did the same in the Kwok family. They became close friends and frequently exchanged views on how they could save some money from the house-keeping to go see the latest American films. Thus, life in school with many other girls created for the lively Daisy a very happy time indeed. She was always smiling. Although slightly plump, she was like a fresh fragrant ball of rising dough. Her mind was filled with ideas, not worries. Life lay before her like a dazzling blue sea. She could go boating or swimming as she pleased.

Chapter Four

1928
Nineteen Years Old

Wearing Chinese Dresses but Speaking English

Something solid and glittering could be detected within this tender and pure young beauty. Something lucent and as sharp as a gem could be sensed sparkling in her eyes.

The McTyeire students' sitting room in the 1920s, furnished by themselves. This is where they practised the role of hostesses as part of their curriculum.

During the week before graduation, teachers and students took part in various forms of celebration. Individual classes held farewell gatherings and there was a graduation "Sunday." This was when all the graduating students wore pure white silk. The day before they said good-bye to the entire school dressed in their class colors, white lined with blue, or blue lined with white. They linked hands and marched through the school grounds to all the main buildings and sites, singing songs of farewell. Finally they reached the great hall where the whole school was assembled, the stage decorated with flowers and flags. Speeches of farewell were read aloud while the graduating students sang their class song and presented gifts to the school. As a representative of the school receiving gifts, I shed tears several times. So did the students.

Usually the graduation ceremony took place the next day. Families, relatives and friends arrived from early morning, bringing flowers that lined both sides of the hall. Greetings and congratulations filled the air. The ceremony began promptly at nine o'clock. Wearing specially made dresses, the graduates entered the hall through the main door and proceeded to the first row as the entire school sang the school song. The graduates then mounted the platform to receive their certificates.

After the ceremony the new graduates and their teachers were photographed together. Many of the flowers were sent to the sick and unwell in hospitals. Finally, the new graduates with their tear-stained faces were seen off by the lower classes.

—From the memoirs of a former principal of McTyeire School for Girls, Xue Zheng

This was how Daisy graduated from middle school in 1928. By then she had already grown into a striking young woman. A yellow and torn photograph reveals her beauty at the time, suggestive of the beauty of Venus in the work of Botticelli. During the winter of 1997 I selected this photo from Daisy's album and asked a photographer to restore it, with a view to including it in this volume. The photographer was from New York and specialized in models whose beauty, he reflected, could only be compared to the freshness of dew. When he looked through a lens at this photograph of Daisy in 1928, he said:

"I have never seen such a tender and lovely woman!"

But what I saw differed from the beauty of models and glittering Venetian scenes. It was the twinkle in her eyes, as translucent as diamonds, but sharper and not revealed before in the photos of her as a child.

Daisy could not recall when this photo was taken. But after

Daisy in a long Chinese gown. When she arrived in Hong Kong after her elder sisters and saw them wearing silk, she thought this type of clothing was most unsuitable for young people.

examining it with an old-fashioned magnifying glass having a black handle, she said:

"I think it must have been after I graduated from McTyeire and started wearing Chinese dresses."

As we looked at the photos together, I often had to ask when a particular one was taken. She always said she had forgotten, then she would say:

"See if I am wearing a Chinese dress. That would be after I graduated."

Later she said if she wore a cheongsam that would be before 1949. If it was a cheongsam cut down to a short blouse that would be after 1949 as it was no longer suitable to go around wearing the cheongsam then. As far as Daisy was concerned, after graduation it was always Chinese style dresses.

So we began with this photo. But one question always bothered me. She graduated from a famous western-style missionary school. Her command of English was impeccable, her knowledge was Americanized, her world outlook was formed in a library of books by world renowned writers. She had never taken part in China's new cultural movement. She had not followed the radical students to collect street donations for the student movement. Instead, she devoted herself to American-style home economics, developing an interest in cake-making, in sports and drama. After she became McTyeire's "model girl," she switched over to wearing elaborate Chinese-style dresses, indulging in the use of silk. Western-style ornaments and imported materials were all the rage then among society women in Shanghai. Trends in Paris and New York reached Shanghai as fast as planes could fly. The result was that many McTyeire students grew up speaking more English than Chinese. They were looked upon as China's most westernized young women. The Soong sisters, after graduating from McTyeire, also adopted Chinese style clothing and Chinese hair-styles.

This is also what happened to Daisy.

I asked about her spontaneous use of the English language. Right up to the time of her death she habitually used English. Even in her last days when I telephoned her, she would say in English:

"I am dying."

With the passing of so many years, she could speak Chinese, including the Shanghai dialect, but she regularly slipped into an English-speaking frame of mind, that of her mother tongue. So I asked her:

"Why did you insist on wearing Chinese dresses?"

It was only during the Cultural Revolution, when Chinese dresses were labeled among "the four olds" to be swept aside, that she changed over to wearing the same blue cotton clothing as others.

Her reply was: "Why? Because I liked to, that's why."

She was unable to produce a reason with grand words.

Despite all her learning directed towards cultivating individual interest, and a wider and just view of the world, her formative years at McTyeire did not turn her into a snobbish admirer of western values while despising eastern ones. Rather she learned the meaning of social justice, discovered beauty, found and took pride in herself. Was this achieved in eight years, not from slogans, but from cultivation from morning till night in a library with no Chinese books and listening to Beethoven and Tsaichovsky evening after evening?

Two directions in life faced the McTyeire graduates: to get married and fulfill their greatest role in life, or to pursue further studies in the wider world of the United States. Daisy had wanted to go to the United States to continue her studies, along with many others, including her good friend Helen Tsang, but Daisy's father saw no point in a girl going to America to study. Thus, seven weeks after she recovered from typhoid fever, she got engaged to the son of a wealthy family, Albert. Albert had graduated from St. John's University and gone to the United States to study. So after Daisy recovered, she was taken to Albert's home in Peking to recuperate. Their fathers were old friends and the thirties scenario of a pretty girl destined to become a graceful young matron began to unfold.

However, the situation quickly changed. In Peking, Daisy discovered the newly-established Yenching University. She decided she wanted to continue her studies in Peking and she broke off her engagement to Albert.

No longer the little girl with the big bow in her hair playing "follow the leader" with Wally, she began to reveal the other side of the diamond in her eyes, the freedom to independently take her own course in life. When Albert returned from America, armed with a revolver, he went to the railway station to intercept Daisy on her way home to Shanghai for the winter holidays. But all his entreaties were to no avail. She no longer liked him, particularly after he had presented her with a pair of American nylon stockings and said:

"These stockings are very hard-wearing, they won't wear out, even in a year."

Many years later, Daisy said:

"I couldn't marry a man who wanted to tell me how hard-wearing nylon stockings were. No fun."

She never considered a family's wealth because she herself never lacked for money. Nor did she consider what the future might hold for an American returned student. As far as she was concerned, everyone around her was assured of a successful future. She did not care whether she was liked or not. She had many suitors in her circle of friends who felt they could never match this fourth daughter of the

A gathering of former McTyeire students after the Cultural Revolution. With the relaxed situation, there was no more danger of being charged with holding illegal gatherings. So these survivors came together again with cakes, coffee and candles.

Kwok family. What she wanted was to share a common language with someone with whom she could have a lot of fun. Not long afterwards she met a graduate of the Massachusetts Institute of Technology who became her future husband. She did not want a boyfriend with whom she had nothing to talk about.

Albert raised his revolver and said he wanted to kill her. She said:

"Even if you don't kill me, I still don't want to marry you. If you kill me I still won't marry you because I won't be able to."

Then he said he wanted to kill himself and she said:

"Go home. You only end up not being able to marry me. If you kill yourself, you will never be able to get married, you won't even have any life left."

That was how Daisy ended her first engagement, putting behind her the conventional thirties story of a meek and mild girl from a well-to-do family.

She next put an end to her years of piano practice. Although this accomplishment was fashionably demanded of younger girls in Shanghai, she did not like the piano.

"I do not want to learn the piano any more," she told Wally the day she closed her piano for good. He was the one who had said:

"Everyone is learning to play the piano, so you must too."

The sound box shook followed by a vague crashing of the keys as Daisy left the ranks of Shanghai's kind and gentle girls.

All this happened after she graduated from McTyeire. From then on she stubbornly followed her own inclination and ideals. Although this was regarded in 1928 as the finickiness of a young and spoilt girl, by 1961 Daisy's husband lay dead in the Tilanqiao Prison Hospital. In 1966 she was driven from her home and had to share an attic with her university student son, and a common toilet with the other residents. In 1972 she used an iron wok on a coal ball stove to make St. Petersburg-style cakes. Yet in 1982 she returned to the farm where she was originally sent to be reformed through labor in order to teach the young people there English. Always looking to the future, in 1985 she drew up the documents donating her remains after death to the Shanghai Red Cross Society. In 1996, many were amazed to discover in conversation with her the wit and liveliness of a young girl that radiated from within her. After Daisy died in 1998, the grand-daughter she had once looked after, and who was already managing a Las Vegas fashion store, touched her hand at the funeral and exclaimed:

"Why is grandma so cold?"

She could not believe that her grandmother would one day die. To her, Daisy was unlike anyone else, the unbending stubbornness in her eyes would continue to radiate.

What then was the relationship between this fierce independence and bravery and the tears and songs of the graduating students at McTyeire?

Sometimes I saw Daisy as a young politically-inclined red who had escaped from a well-to-do family and whose ideals had brought her close to revolution. There have always been such stories of idealistic people. They differed from those who pursued revolution for the sake of enough to eat, to escape marriage or change society. Instead they pursued the justice and ideals they learned from books. Daisy was not a revolutionary. She wanted to live her own life and pursue her own ideals, greatly valuing individual rights. She was one of those girls photographed with two lilies behind her shoulder.

When Daisy's house was searched someone poked a hole in the photo and left it lying on the ground. It was picked up by Daisy's sister, Pearlie. In all the confusion that followed Daisy did not know how it got to Singapore and was kept by relatives there. In 1987, after visiting her family in the United States, she went to Singapore to see her husband's relatives. There she was given an album of photos collected for her. The relatives there knew her own albums had been destroyed. It was in this collection that she saw this photo again.

Chapter Five

1931
Twenty-two Years Old

The Big House in Lucerne Road

Sitting before her worn green curtain, Daisy scooped her hands to draw the air towards her. Her eyes half-closed, her head raised, she said: "Can you smell the osmanthus? How sweet it is!"

*I*t was dusk one evening in 1997. Daisy and I were sitting and chatting before the big window in her room. She loved this window, overlooking the peaceful lane outside that was swathed in the greenery of the trees that gave off the faint aroma of cassia in the autumn air. It was one of those fine autumn evenings to be found in various corners of Shanghai. She corrected some of my English with a smile that was both encouraging and apologetic, typical of an overly fond mother with a child who had fallen into the water. She had a way of expressing herself that could never be misunderstood.

We were enjoying a chocolate cake sent over by a French lady. By then Daisy had a room in an apartment, which she shared with someone else. But although it was supplied with gas, there was no oven. She was extremely frugal. Her grand-daughter, Mae, sent her beautiful clothes each year but she put them away without wearing them. In the winter she carried around an old-fashioned quartz heater with which she had singed her woolen sweaters and slacks. In the olden days she had grown up in a big house and together with relatives and friends had learned the art of making cakes, chocolate and maraschino cherries from an émigré chef from the Czarist household, probably the most expensive cooking course going at the time. This was why others thought she had been unfairly treated and tried to make up for what she had lost. There was always somebody who sent her a home-made cake, carefully wrapped in silver paper. Others took her out for meals and again someone would note any preference she showed and order an extra portion for her to take home for dinner. Truly acts of compassion!

During the nineties when Shanghai began to restore much of its old self, an old photo of Daisy's family taken in front of their large house, was featured in many publications. Included was a copperplate

The George Kwok Bew family, once held as the ideal model of a well-to-do family. After a lapse of 70 years, the youth of Shanghai have once again turned their attention to this yellowed, torn and burned old photo.

magazine catering for white collar workers. It was so finely printed that even the yellowed four corners of the pages could be clearly seen. One writer said that Shanghai people looking at that photo could not determine whether they had returned to the past or arrived in the future.

In any case, all wanted to eradicate all memories of a destructive period in their lives and return to the atmosphere of this group photo. In doing so, they could imagine they too were living in a big house, the women wearing long gowns, their nephews dressed like little English boys, with neatly tied neckties, the fathers earning good money along Nanjing Road. Or they themselves were attending Yenching University and returning home for the summer holidays, when they would ride with brothers and sisters in the family Buick to catch the breeze.

The newspapers were filled then with advertisements for holiday homes. Along Avenue Joffre shops with well-known western names stood side by side. One café even selected "1931" for its name, indicative of this longing for a return to Shanghai's halcyon days. One was reminded of the legendary King of Corinth, Sisyphus, who was condemned to roll a heavy rock up a hill, only to have it roll down again as it neared the top. In Daisy's case, it was during this upheaval that she lost her past.

According to Daisy, nothing in this world lasted. Like water, once it stopped flowing, it dried up.

She once had a good friend, a beautiful woman, who was planning to celebrate her fortieth birthday and invited Daisy to join her. Daisy arrived at her home at the appointed time but her friend was not there. Daisy had to wait a long time for her return. She explained she had been to the photographer's because after one's fortieth birthday one should not be photographed any more as from then on one became old. She thought by keeping a few photos she could retain something. However, when the Cultural Revolution came, her photos were burned.

"I had more than 30 photo albums," said Daisy, "and all were torn up. Nothing can be kept in this world."

I remember her sitting before the window. The light was shining on her, showing the smile on her face, no trace at all of any hurt.

People today who still dream of a life like that reflected in the Kwok family photo are rather like the fox mourning the death of the hare. But if they examine their consciences in the still of the night they will realize they would not be able to endure all that Daisy went through.

Daisy said she once dreamed that the Cultural Revolution had returned. Her house was sacked and sealed. Then she woke up. She

The newly-built Wing On Department Store in 1918. This white western-style building along Nanjing Road symbolized the maturing of the national capitalists' department store industry.

asked herself if the Cultural Revolution really returned would she be able to go through it again?

"I decided I could," she declared. "Then I thought about my children. Could they? I decided yes, if I could they could too and they would be all right."

"But you lost so much." I reminded her.

"I learned so much." she replied. "If I had gone on living in the same way as when I was a little girl, I would never have known how big my heart could become, that I could put up with so much. I feel now that I have lived a very full life, which most people never experience."

These are facts, an individual's awareness of the reality of the world. From that time on I became very fond of Daisy and talking with her. I thrilled at the sound of her deep voice. She always pressed me to take some food with me whenever I left. They were gifts that others had brought and were piled up high in the cupboard beside the door. She would say:

"I don't know why they always want to give me things. I can't possibly make use of it all. Some people even want to give me money. I don't need any."

Very often it was those who hungered for those beautiful things who imagined she wanted them even more. We have a habit of assuming that people can move from poverty to riches but never the other way round.

"Why do people want money so much? They're all talking about money," she said. She raised her eyebrows as she went on.

"I had riches before, then I lost them. I really don't think it's important. I have never thought money was important."

Daisy particularly liked this group photo of the Kwok family. It was the best that the family now had left. She pointed out to me the wing of the house where her bedroom used to be. That's how I knew the big house with the white windows was always in her mind. She spent her happiest days there. One by one, she told me about each member of the family. I realized her emotional attachment to these people. They were her own flesh and blood. She treasured everything in that photo because that was where she came from. Younger generations of the Kwok family living abroad were then frequently visiting Shanghai and Daisy took them to see the old house in Lucerne Road. By then 37 families were housed there. She wanted them to see what the old house was like. She showed them the hothouse, just like when she visited Australia in March 1990 when she was 80, and wanted to retrace her own roots.

Had Daisy been unhappy with the pity shown her, or was hoping the old house in Lucerne Road would be returned to the original owners, had she said she did not care about money and spoke in a dry voice like Ah Q, then I would have understood what she really thought. But it wasn't like that. She simply regarded the pity as well-meaning but unnecessary. While some entertained groundless fears for her, in fact she was living under a bright blue sky with light clouds and breezes.

Sometimes, such famous Chinese phrases as "an upright person who is neither intimidated by force nor subdued by wealth or rank", or "one who remains firm in his principles despite poverty" would enter my mind. But I hesitate in applying these phrases to Daisy, for it would be like mixing cabbage and spinach in the same pot.

Then how to portray her?

I can't help thinking of that autumn evening with the warm evening breeze. Daisy sat before the faded green curtains, gently scooping the air towards her, her head tilted upwards, her eyes half closed and exclaiming in delight:

"Can you smell the cassia? How sweet it is!"

Chapter Six

1932
Twenty-three Years Old

Father Died

George Kwok Bew, one of the founders of the Wing On
Department Store in Shanghai.

*E*arly in January 1932 Daisy's father, George Kwok Bew, unexpectedly fell ill and died in the home of Yi Tai Tai (courtesy title accorded to a concubine). His death was so sudden that he left no will or instructions, but a considerable sum in assets. He was buried on 6th January 1932.

The Kwok family decided to divide the estate in accordance with their father's past practice of giving each son two shares and each daughter one. They invited Yi Tai Tai and her children to meet with them, intending to make provision for them. But Yi Tai Tai explained that George Kwok Bew had already provided for them and they did not want any further share of the estate.

Presumably this unusual equalitarianism sprang from a deep sense of pride and dignity. Sixty-six years later, Daisy's daughter, Jingshu, could proudly give the details.

During this year Daisy was a third-year student in the department of psychology at Yenching University. She became interested in child psychology and also became a shareholder in the Shanghai Wing On Company.

Chapter Seven

1933

Twenty-four Years Old

Yenching University Student

Jingshu, Daisy's daughter, said she thought her mother's bearing came from the education she received at Yenching University. Sometimes when in Daisy's company, I myself would feel an urge to find the time to take lessons in ballet for adults.

$\mathcal{T}$he last time I saw Daisy was September 24th, 1998, at the end of summer, once again at dusk. Her white hair had been set and she had painted her lips red, like the exquisite woman she was, with no sign of red on her teeth. From the time we first met she had always made up her face every time she had a visitor by appointment. By contrast, my generation only paid such attention to their appearance for someone they considered important, usually a man, and mostly with the intention to please. But Daisy did so out of courtesy.

Her old houseboy, Songlin, was also present that day. Daisy was already very weak and Songlin had left his home and come to Shanghai to take care of his former mistress. He lived in a small room at the back of the apartment. Daisy asked Songlin to fetch two things to show me. He had found them while tidying up. One of these was an enlarged photograph in a frame, taken after her graduation from Yenching University.

This photo, Daisy told me, had been taken by the photographer next to the Park Hotel. Passing by some time afterwards, Daisy discovered the enlargement was on display in the photographer's window. She had entered the shop and taken the photo down, saying:

"Who gave you permission to display this photo for all to see?"

The shop owner realized he was at fault and presented the photo to her, by way of apology. Daisy took the photo home but soon afterwards it disappeared.

In fact, the photo did not resurface until the Cultural Revolution ended. It was returned to her by relatives of her deceased husband. They had cautiously arrived back in Shanghai to visit remaining relatives there. Using the same keys from thirty years before, they had opened the door of their old home and found the photo in the room once occupied by Daisy's husband. It was the first photo returned to

Sometimes, when looking at the photos of Daisy's student days, one wonders what sort of a life would match this perfect child.

Daisy after the Cultural Revolution.

Already in her seventies, only then did Daisy learn how the photo had been stolen from her home.

"How on earth was he able to move such an enormous thing from our house? No one in our house, including the gateman, found out." Daisy said, touching my hand to indicate how odd it was that this was the only photo of her left intact in Shanghai.

She marveled with delight at the audacity of this clever young man, this master of new fads. That was how she had fallen in love and married this one-time Tsinghua University student. The photo was undiscovered because in 1949 the house where it was had been locked up. By 1949 Daisy already had two children and had been Mrs. Woo for fifteen years. When she saw this photo again the young man who had stolen it had been dead for twenty years.

The second item Daisy wanted to show me was her graduation certificate from Yenching University. Both served as records of Daisy's days at Yenching. During the 1930s it was all the rage for girls from Yenching University to marry boys from Tsinghua. Former students of these universities would nod their heads knowingly when they heard the story.

While Daisy did not work in her specialized field she drew on her knowledge of psychology during the 1940s in dealing with her own children and those of other families. Even during the nineties the oldest of these recalled their childhood days with the "fairy-like" Auntie Daisy, claiming that she knew how to make them happy.

In the 1950s Daisy had to contend with a great deal of hostility towards her and her family. When her husband was jailed and the police confronted her with accusations from all sides, she pretended to have a poor knowledge of Chinese in order to gain the time taken by the interpreting to size up the situation. When she went to see her sister

Daisy Kwok graduation certificate from Yenching University.

Pearlie, the only other member of her family remaining in Shanghai, Daisy was knocked to the ground by the red guards waiting outside to search Pearlie's house. Finding herself unable to call to Pearlie to come out, Daisy feigned an attack of high blood pressure to frighten the red guards. Just before her retirement when she realized the red guards were about to mount one last tongue-lashing on the assembled capitalist elements before they were sent home, she made a speech in which she said retirement would allow her to have more time to study Chinese so that she could read and understand Mao's works better and remold herself further. Starting from the age of 11, Zhongzheng began to observe how his mother dealt with the hardship in life. He revealed how profoundly he was affected by the way she lived. Even today, his eyes moisten and redden as he smiles and says:

"Mother studied psychology. She knew how to protect herself. She used to say my father was smart but he only knew how to enjoy himself. She was the clever one."

Daisy often recalled her days at Yenching. When she was 49, she and other staff members of foreign trade who were considered to be of capitalist background, were sent to the affiliated farm to work. There was virtually nothing at the farm then. The farm buildings were just being put up and all hands were put to work on the building site. But already in their mid-forties, they dared not climb the bamboo scaffolding. They stood there petrified while they were jeered at and ordered to move. Just then Daisy emerged carrying a bucket of cement mixture and proceeded to climb up.

That evening she returned home very pleased with herself. She told Zhongzheng:

"I was able to do what the others couldn't. I wasn't afraid. My hands and feet are still very flexible."

She always saw the "fun" side of the situation, after which she would describe what happened to her son who was worrying by himself at home. It was through these stories of "fun" that he had some idea of what she was going through. But he remembered with pride how his mother had captained the North China Women's Tennis Team, and how she had always liked sports.

Daisy remained independent right up to the day she died. She was already 88 when I got to know her. She was then doing her own shopping every day. She would not be home when I telephoned her on fine, sunny days. She would be out for a walk and one day I went with her. Standing as straight as a ramrod, she slowly and elegantly walked under the shade of the trees. She reminded me of the fragrance of an English cup of tea before the milk is added. While she was at Yenching, in order to take part in the Peking Opera *You Lung Xi Feng* (Emperor Meets Girl) in English, she practiced walking with a hard-cover book on her head. Jingshu believed that her mother's deportment was acquired at Yenching. Sometimes when I was in Daisy's company I would feel an urge to make time to take lessons in ballet for adults.

One day as Daisy and I were passing a supermarket, she told me that an elderly gentleman had accosted her and said he would like to make friends with her. She sometimes revealed a slight irritation in her speech, like a maiden, fearing to be mixed up with men she did not know. I laughed and put my arm round her. I told her if I was 88 and an elderly man crossed the street to talk to me I would feel as if I had won a medal!

Chapter Eight

1934
Twenty-five Years Old

Parting

Daisy returned from Peking to Shanghai in 1934. Already she regarded Shanghai as her home. The man she loved was in Shanghai. Her future home would be there and so she believed Shanghai would become her future paradise.

This photo of Daisy, Wally and Elsie Kwok was taken in 1934 as Daisy prepared for her engagement.

*B*efore they left Australia, the younger members of the family were photographed with their eldest sister, Edie. At the time, Daisy had no idea what Shanghai would be like. Wally was then a mischievous little boy. Elsie was already promising to develop into the beautiful girl that would be selected as the first Miss Shanghai. They were a lively lot of children, occupying themselves each day as they wished, without thought of the future, as was usually the case with children of families living in favorable circumstances. This was the carefree way in which Daisy and her siblings grew up.

By 1934 Daisy was about to become formally engaged and had permed her hair for the occasion. Already she looked upon Shanghai as her home, the man she loved was in Shanghai and she believed

Shanghai would become her future paradise.

Daisy's view of Shanghai in 1934 was a glowing scene of stability and affection. Little did she realize that Shanghai was where her heart would be broken, that she would one day lose her home there. Nor could she foresee that one night while travelling on the No. 71 bus route from the farm at the eastern end of this sprawling city to her home at the west end she would be so tired that she slept past her stop and was carried on to the terminus, that after alighting from the bus, she would tear wildly about to try and reach her teenage son waiting at home for her return. She was not then required to live on the farm where she had been sent to reform herself through labor. Eventually she did manage to find her way through the midnight darkness. Even then, however, she still had no idea that Shanghai was to become her real home. By the time of her final years though, no matter where she went, including to her daughter's home in Peking, she would become unsettled after a few months and hanker to return to Shanghai.

Probably realizing that her forthcoming engagement in 1934 was not going to be the same as an earlier one she had broken off with Albert, Daisy arranged to be photographed with Wally and Elsie. Sooner or later they would leave their family home and their days of living together would end. Although Wally was already married, his wife did not join them. Thus the three of them presented their smiling faces before the camera.

They must have recalled a similar situation after leaving Australia for the Far East. For the first time in Hong Kong, they encountered a strange smell they had never come across before. They came across the same heavy odor in a hotel in Shanghai. Only later did they find out it was the smell of opium. Life was never the same again after that.

Their photo taken in 1934 marked a parting of the ways for them. Wally who took up racing cars in Shanghai finally settled down to a quiet life in the United States. Daisy, who never did anything improper in her life, learned what it was like to be the wife of a capitalist in Red China. Her husband was subsequently jailed for illegal foreign exchange dealings, while the second half of her life there was turned into a soul-stirring experience.

Chapter Nine

April 1934
Twenty-five Years Old

A Beautiful but Stubborn Girl Marries

Their bottom line in the pursuit of life was happiness. They scorned ordinary life while arrogantly allowing no compromise or deference to it.

Daisy's engagement was announced at a garden party hosted by her mother. Perhaps her mother did not approve of her choice of the descendant of a poor scholar, but Daisy was determined and the family accepted Daisy's choice.

*D*aisy's engagement was announced at a garden party in the Kwok family home. She wore a large pair of pearl earrings and a long gown that had four loops for buttons on the collar. More than 200 tables of guests were present. This was how she joined the family of her beloved one and how he who secretly removed her photo from the Kwok family residence won a beautiful woman.

Her husband, Woo Yu-hsiang, was a descendant of the Fuzhou family of Lin Zexu. Commissioner Lin Zexu (1785–1850) was sent to Guangdong by the Emperor of China in March 1839 to suppress the opium trade. Woo's mother's grandmother was a daughter of Lin Zexu. By the time Woo was born his family had been a poor but honest family for generations. Traditionally, when a poor scholar won an appointment through the official examinations the rest of his family would not have had much education. Thus the children were taught by their elders to study the sacred books. While these children mostly grew up to be scholars they were weak physically. It was the next generation with no previous official status who became the true scholars. They had light complexions, long fingers and were bursting with new ideas. Often refined but not practical, they resembled the sweet-smelling cigarettes that provided pleasurable refreshment.

Woo Yu-hsiang was one of these. Later the Woo family remarked that Daisy's family had a higher status. But Daisy never said anything like this.

When Woo was 19 he was awarded a Boxer Indemnity Fund scholarship. He was admitted to the preparatory department for students being sent to the United States just at the time the May Fourth Movement exploded among students in Peking. He took part in the

The Tsinghua University preparatory class for students awarded scholarships to study in the United States. Reflecting the defiant spirit of the May Fourth Movement's outburst, their young faces also show some doubt. Did they really understand what they were doing?

demonstrations held by the university students until he was arrested. Daisy was then 10, happily studying in English at an American Protestant primary school housed in the Moore Memorial Church. But she became annoyed when her sisters forced her to wear western-style hats.

Fearing that the scholarship students had forgotten their responsibility to their benefactors and would become uncontrollable, in 1921 it

Woo Yu-hsiang at the Massachusetts Institute of Technology. His fate in the cloudy distant south-east of China still awaited him.

was decided to send off this batch of students to the United States ahead of time. Woo was sent to the Massachusetts Institute of Technology to major in electrical engineering and sub-major in industrial management. Before the students left, a group photograph of them was taken outside the building housing their department. Among this class of mostly young male students wearing soft long padded gowns, this young Fuzhou student still retained the spirit of the slogan, "Down with Confucius."

However, not long after his arrival in the eastern United States he was transformed into a Chinese man smartly dressed in western clothes. Outside of his studies, he quickly developed an interest in American sports, particularly baseball. During the 1950s, when the

United States became China's No. 1 enemy, listening to American radio broadcasts was grounds for arrest. But Woo could not resist turning the volume low, his tall frame bent over the loudspeaker, trying to cut through the jamming to hear the baseball results as well as the live commentary. He turned out to be the type of student the government had hoped for when the scholarships were awarded. While in America he forgot about politics. Probably he joined the May Fourth demonstrations because they provided a new stimulus. When he graduated from MIT, not only had he become a master of new fads, but was striving to make perfection even more perfect, like the fragrant cigarettes indulged in by many idle women.

Daisy was then rehearsing Shakespeare's plays in McTyeire School's drab-colored hall. Sixty years later, when she went to America, during the quiet days when she was writing her memoirs, she commented on her play-acting, saying "It was fun."

After Woo Yu-hsiang returned to China, he first took on a teaching job at Tsinghua University. But he soon decided the academics there were too dull. He resigned and returned to his home in the Hongkew district in Shanghai. He decided to seek his fortune in business instead and joined the managerial staff of a foreign-owned dairy farm. He wore fashionable western clothes all the year round, was extremely western in his life-style, returning home to sleep after midnight. His family found a girl for him to marry and he gave her 300 yuan to go shopping and buy whatever she liked. The girl bought stacks of cotton printed cloth and a selection of face powders and rouge. Woo's reaction was to break off the engagement, saying:

"How can I put up with such a woman?"

This was about the same time that Daisy broke off her engagement to Albert in Peking because he said that nylon stockings were hard-wearing and he was no fun.

Clearly Daisy and Woo's marriage was not based on a desire to spend their lives sharing a common goal. While they both sought happiness, they scorned ordinary life and were determined not to make any compromise. Thus by March 15th, 1958, Woo Yu-hsiang's last day of freedom, he was still driving his Ford to work. The majority of capitalists had already put away their cars and were riding in pedicabs. Daisy and her son had to drive the Ford home after Woo was arrested.

Four years later, in September 1962, Daisy was working on a farm for the purpose of remoulding herself through labor, when she received a notification from the public security bureau to return to Shanghai and await further instructions. Daisy's workmates, fearing she might get lost, urged her to notify her family how she would be travelling. Nevertheless, she took a small boat by herself that meandered along a green-colored river in the countryside. Many years later she still recalled this trip, how green and beautiful it was.

Daisy and Woo's engagement photo, taken on the Kwok family garden steps in 1934, reveals their smiling hearts at the time. However, fifty years later in 1980, Daisy stood alone on the same steps. The first step had already sunken into the ground while the ashes of the one beside her had disappeared in 1967. Daisy was still wearing a long gown. Her hair was freshly set but had turned white. A careful look at this photo with a magnifying glass revealed some of the vicissitudes in her life.

In her final years, Daisy said:

"Youth is really a test. I realize now how deeply I hurt Albert and his parents. I stayed with them for nearly one year. If they looked upon me as an evil person I would not blame them."

Chapter Ten

November 1934
Twenty-five Years Old

A Story of Love

Her self-esteem, her grace and her restraint appeared to hide a wound caused by disloyalty. The husband she had fallen in love with was really amiable, but perhaps he wanted more than ordinary family life.

At the end of 1934 a beautiful girl fulfilled her dream of marrying a man with whom she could really communicate. There is not the slightest doubt of this on her face.

A young television producer became interested in Daisy's story. He thought to turn it into a 20-part serial. Pouring his well-groomed head over Daisy's wedding photo, he muttered to himself:

"... Too beautiful. No, no, it won't do, a woman born under an unlucky star ..."

The wedding photographer was Skvirsky, the best of all the White Russian photographers in Shanghai. His seal could still be seen in the right hand corner.

Daisy looks like the princess in *Roman Holiday*, so tender, innocent, majestic and happy as she prepares to face the future, with no thought of anything but the golden apple before her. That is, except for her fears about their first breakfast.

This is what she wrote in her memoirs:

From the day we were engaged until the wedding day, six months later, I was so busy planning everything for a new home. There was furniture to be bought or ordered, drapes, bed linen, carpets, kitchen appliances, chinaware, and the engagement of reliable servants. The guest list had to be made and invitations sent out, and there was my clothing, most important of all—my wedding gown. It was no wonder I lost weight and was only eighty-eight pounds by the time I thought I had done everything.

The night before the wedding I suddenly wondered what we should have for breakfast the next day. I had no idea what my husband-to-be (I called him YH) was in the habit of eating. We had had lunches, teas, dinners and suppers together, but never breakfast, and as far as I could recall, we had never even discussed such things.

"Well, I'll have to plan something," I thought, "I can't let him find me a very incompetent housewife."

My brain was twirling around. Should I serve a Chinese breakfast of congee (rice porridge) with its accompanying dishes of shredded meat, pickled cucumbers, peanuts, black eggs, bean curd etc., or would he prefer a foreign style meal? Then I remembered the continental or English breakfast I had been served in hotels I had stayed in Manila or Hong Kong. I thought I couldn't go wrong if I did something like that.

I got up early the next morning to give my cook instructions on what to prepare for the first meal in our new home. When it was ready I laid the table myself, and then called my husband, announcing that breakfast was ready.

When we were seated at the table I started off with fresh orange juice, then porridge with milk and sugar, next bacon and eggs with toast, butter and marmalade and finally ending with coffee with thick cream and sugar. I hardly ate anything.

Daisy Kwok and Woo Yu-hsiang's wedding photo in 1934.

I was so busy serving him. At the end of the meal I looked at him anxiously and asked, "Did you like it? Tell me, what do you usually have for breakfast?"

"Oh this was fine," he said, "but actually I only have a glass of milk with a raw egg beaten in it for breakfast. What are you in the habit of eating?"

"Oh," I replied, "I only drink a cup of coffee."

What a relief it was to know I wouldn't have to go through the ordeal of preparing such a breakfast again.

The young television producer raised his head from the yellowing photograph and said:

"The story's too proper. It won't excite the viewers. Tell me, is there another love story inside it, for example, Daisy falling in love with someone else, a triangle or even a quadrilateral?"

I said I didn't think so.

"You see, in those families after eating their fill they have nothing to do so they indulge themselves. It's normal," he said.

Daisy once said something about a meeting held to criticize her during the Cultural Revolution. A fellow staff member stood up and said that before 1949, whenever Daisy went shopping at the Wing On Company, she would sit on a sofa with a cup of tea in one hand and a cigarette in the other. Meanwhile the salesgirls paraded before her holding up new stock. If she nodded they would wrap up whatever it was she wanted. She would then book it up, jump into her new American car and leave. It sounded like a scene from a drama, Daisy said.

There was a tendency in Shanghai society for those who ranked on a lower scale to look upon the layer above as domineering and libertarian. Daisy said that not even in her wildest dreams would she have dared do anything like that. Had she done so she would have been swept out of the family home long ago. Far from ever wanting to behave like that, the education she received at home was even stricter than that in any family with limited connections.

My own impression was that Daisy was not very interested in relations between the sexes. While she talked a lot about her own affairs, she said very little about love or about her husband. Even in her memoirs she wrote just one sentence:

"In 1934 I married YHW."

Once, when I persisted, she said:

"I was attracted to my husband because he was very stimulating company."

She was not like the westernized type of woman we might imagine, wearing lipstick and rouge and chasing after others with honeyed words. Instead she was warm and gentle.

"There must have been a story behind her husband," the TV producer insisted.

This was also my impression. I detected pain behind her self-esteem, grace and restraint. She fell in love with her husband at first sight, but he was not a man to be satisfied with ordinary home life. In 1943 when their son, Zhongzheng, was born, Daisy had a very difficult time lasting more than 2 days. At the time, their daughter, Jingshu, was at home convalescing from pneumonia. But her husband still went to his club to play cards before returning home late at night. This was a husband who brought her happiness but who could not shoulder the responsibilities of a husband. He created the music in Daisy's heart but could not provide her with the life-giving grain.

When I was unable to sleep in kindergarten, I would scratch a hole in the wall with my fingernails, very small at first, until it was large enough to allow a small finger to finally enter. Then a piece of the wall would fall down, exposing a green brick inside. I used this same approach to explore Daisy's affections, starting with a very small hole.

She began by telling me how her Dad's Yi Tai Tai once came to the big house to see her mother. Daisy did not like her because she had taken away her father, so she stood on the staircase and watched Yi Tai Tai. Yi Tai Tai said nothing and went upstairs to find Daisy's mother. Daisy silently waited until Yi Tai Tai came downstairs again. She stopped and said:

"Your mother knows I am the only one she has to worry about, but I have to be on guard against all women."

As Daisy went through life she came to understand what Yi Tai Tai meant and developed friendly relations with her and her children.

Zhongzheng remembered when he was very small his father fell ill and was placed in the Kwang Hua Private Hospital. He and Daisy went together to visit him. An argument took place between Daisy and his father. It was the first time that the parents displayed their unhappiness before the children. Zhongzheng said he did not know why his father cried but his mother did not.

Finally the green brick wall that was blocking Daisy's married life became exposed. One Shanghai evening in the 1940s, Pearlie's husband accompanied Daisy to the home of an unconventional young widow. He was a fellow student of Woo Yu-hsiang's in the preparatory class at Tsinghua University for scholarship students going abroad. Daisy called her husband out and took him home. The young widow was not unknown to Daisy's family. During the war years they and their friends gathered at each other's homes to have a meal, play cards and fraternize. When the widow's husband died, Daisy's family went to the Bubbling Well Temple to be present as he was given the last rites.

Did Daisy drive to the young widow's house in her family's black Ford or someone else's car? None of us know. How did she discover her husband's secret? Did she sneak a look at his drawer or follow him? Or did someone else tell her? We don't know. Seeing that the husband she had chosen was enjoyed by someone else she had to go and fetch him home. Was she heart-broken or did she just feel sorry for herself? Did she feel furious and humiliated? Neither Zhong-zheng nor Jingshu know because Daisy never spoke about this, never made it clear, never took revenge, never exposed it. Her solicitude for others was meticulous. Was it the old-style of womanly tolerance or was it out of despair over a man who could not settle down? Did she realize that to deal with this man of her own choice who was always on the move, she would have to arm herself with the daring of a kite cord? We will never know.

I imagine that when she pressed the bell of the widow's house she would have raised her eyebrows and looked straight at her. Then tossing her head Daisy would have said:

"I am looking for my husband."

The light from the hall would have lit up her face that was still as beautiful as at her wedding.

Going to the Woo home was always a treat for the children of both the Kwok and Woo families. Right up to the day of the memorial service for Daisy, elderly ones with snow-white hair recalled the Woo home at the time. They said the Woo family was always a picture to look at, so dignified and so fortunate. Their home was warm and cosy, the family dog was so handsome, the Christmas tree so large. The Fuzhou chef's dishes were so genuine. Only in a Hollywod film could such perfection be found.

They maintained that had there been no 1949 Daisy would certainly have lived a Hollywood existence. Life would never have become so simple, unlike the television films with their penchant for excessive sentimentality.

Chapter Eleven

1935
Twenty-six Years Old

Dream of a Girl from a Well-to-do Family

As a modern woman ambitious to establish her own career, and not just to serve her husband, for the first time Daisy now showed her will to lead an independent life.

*W*hile visiting the United States in 1990, she did a university writing course at which the instructor asked the students to write about the most moving events in their lives. This is how Daisy recalled her life in Shanghai in 1935:

A friend of mine, Helen Tsang, had returned from New York. We hadn't seen each other since she had left Shanghai while we were classmates in high school. That was in 1927 and it was now 1935. I thought Helen had become quite Bohemian. She dressed differently. She used black nail polish and painted the tips of her nails green. Helen suggested we open a dress salon. She had studied dress designing in New York. She would design the gowns and I was to be the manager.

We rented a room in the Park Hotel and set up our studio. We called it "Tsingyi." This sounded like her Chinese name, but it wasn't the same two characters. These two characters meant "Brocaded Rainbow." We used entirely Chinese materials, and our main clientele was foreign tourists visiting China. We assured our clients that Helen's designs were for each individual customer and guaranteed that no two gowns would be the same.

We scouted all the silk shops in the city searching for materials. We learned a lot about Shanghai, finding treasures in small shops in the most unexpected lanes or alleys. Then we planned to go to Hangzhou, one of the chief silk manufacturing cities in China. There we hoped to buy some gowns made for the officials of the Ching Dynasty. Helen was good at using these gowns to make modern evening gowns. Hangzhou had so much to offer. It was just a matter of being able to locate what we needed.

A friend of YH (my husband) was taking his girl friend to Hangzhou for a holiday and invited us to share his car. It was so much nicer traveling by car but the door on the left hand side of the front seat had something wrong with it. It couldn't be opened from the outside. Each time I got in I complained that it was such a nuisance and told him he should have it fixed. YH drove as he was familiar with the roads. Helen and I sat in the front with him. Arriving at Hangzhou we left the couple and went about our purchases, meeting them the next day for the homeward trip.

It was already dusk when we set off. As we drew near to Shanghai we came to a bridge. When the car reached the top of the slope I noticed some men waving for us to stop. I thought they were the police wishing to inspect the car, but then I noticed one of them was holding a gun and they were not dressed in police uniforms. Our friend in the back seat called out:

"Drive on YH, I believe this is a hold-up."

Before YH could step on the gas one of the men tried to open the door. It would not open. I thanked my lucky stars it was out of order. This was one time I did not complain. We started to drive on. The bandits were infuriated and fired at us. I had my face pressed against the wind-shield. The bullet went through the glass, but it was bullet proof and there was only a small hole. However, the glass splinters covered my face.

I looked at Helen and cried:

"You are bleeding!"

She looked at me and said,

"You are dripping blood!"

The bandits fired two more shots after us, but we were already out of range. We picked up speed and headed for the nearest hospital as soon as we reached Shanghai. I had 23 cuts on my face, and the glass splinters had to be removed, otherwise no serious damage was done. The bullet had passed over my head and went out of the ceiling of the car.

Then we felt hungry and went to Jimmy's Kitchen (a popular steakhouse in downtown Shanghai) for a bite. While there I had a brain wave. Here was a chance to get some publicity for our Tsingyi Salon. I telephoned all the English newspapers in town and asked if they wanted a story, if so come over to Jimmy's Kitchen and get it. Next morning we were in print with a picture of the car and arrows pointing to the bullet holes, and of course Tsingyi Dress Salon at the Park

Hotel got a mention.

When Daisy visited New York in 1990 she saw again her old middle school friend, Helen, whom she had not seen for 53 years. The two elderly ladies met in a Fifth Avenue coffee shop and had much to say to each other. Before they parted, knowing that Daisy had lost all her old newspaper clippings in the Cultural Revolution, Helen presented her with a set of

Daisy's enchanting smile at that time

the Tsingyi Fashion Salon clippings, including a copy of a letter from the husband of one of their customers, thanking them for making her look so beautiful.

Nobody knows about the Tsingyi Fashion Salon today. Nor does anyone realize that they once created a modern women's designer salon, using Chinese materials to produce women's formal wear. No one realizes that their ideal was to create modern Chinese women's formal wear, traversing a path that followed neither the styles of Paris nor those of Peiping. Daisy photocopied all those 1936 newspaper clippings about the opening fashion shows put on by the salon and that had been so carefully saved by Helen.

Report by the *Ta Kung Pao*

Fashion Show at Park Hotel Today

From tomorrow until the 6th, a fashion show will be held by the Tsingyi Fashion Salon every afternoon from five to seven on the third floor of the Park Hotel. The salon was recently established by Kuomintang Eminence Tsang Tsing-kiang's eldest daughter, Tsang Tsing-yi. The salon commences business tomorrow at 405 The Park Hotel, on Bubbling Well Road. In order to make known the work of the salon, a priceless collection of garments, totally unlike current fashions in Shanghai and each individually designed by Miss Tsang, will be displayed. Shanghai's leading dress designer, Miss Tsang personally does all the designing, while Miss Guo Wanying, a graduate of Peiping's Yenching University, is in charge of management.

Report by Ziyan from *Current Affairs*

Glimpses of the Tsingyi Dress Salon's Fashion Show

(1) As the curtain of night descends the neon lights shine bright and coquettish. On the streets, a cool autumn wind is blowing the leaves about and filling the poor with despair. Where are they to obtain autumn clothing for the cooler weather?

But on the fourth floor of the Park Hotel it is warm. An afternoon tea gathering is taking place. Lights from the four walls shine on the tea tables. One forgets the falling leaves and autumn breezes. Well-dressed women and young ladies rest on the sofas, sipping tea and smoking at their leisure.

Their well-manicured hands dexterously balance flickering cigarettes under the bright lights. The rising smoke envelops their faces in a slight haze. The tempting fragrance of the coffee and cake and the warm atmosphere create a sense of drowsiness, the tinkling of the piano adding rhythm to the conversation.

Although most of the exquisitely dressed ladies were Chinese, they spoke to each other in impeccable English. Those already seated welcomed the later arrivals in upper crust fashion:

"Oh Mary, how are you!"

Wearing their own styles of dress and speaking in their own patterns of English, the newcomers responded by extending their well-manicured hands and

Tsingyi fashions

painted red nails for a mutual shake.

(2) In an address to those present, a Mr.Hu explained that the purpose of the gathering was to mark the recent establishment of Miss Tsang Tsing-ying's Tsingyi Dress Salon. He said the salon intended to promote the use of Chinese fabrics and materials among fashion circles in both Chinese and Western society. Until then, well-to-do Chinese women had preferred to use expensive imported materials costing one to two hundred yuan. Miss Tsang wanted to spread the use of Chinese materials, at a much lower price. At the same time, should Western women and girls like the Chinese materials, a greater return could be earned from them. Miss Tsang thought Chinese fashions were too conservative, while Western fashions were too flamboyant. She wanted to blend the two with no loss of their beauty or naturalness.

Miss Tsang was a graduate of McTyeire School for Girls, Mr. Hu said, and had studied fashion in the United States. Her purpose in returning to China was not that she wanted to transform fashions. But she did have an interest in fashion. Recently many of her friends had asked her to design clothes for them, for example, the movie star, Huang Liu-shuang, and others equally well-known. That was how she came to set up the Tsingyi Dress Salon

The difference between Miss Tsang's salon and other fashion houses was that Miss Tsang's designs were based on the physique and individuality of the individual. No two garments were alike nor were their prices. The few items on display ranged between fifty and eighty yuan. If imported materials were used the price would be about one hundred yuan but compared with overseas designers this was still much lower.

(3) The fashion show began in this warm atmosphere.

Spotlights from two corners embellished the two models, one Chinese and the other a Westerner. They displayed 8 designs between them. Exclamations of delight greeted their appearance. After they circled around the onlookers, another burst of applause sent them on their way.

Circling around repeatedly to the obvious approval of the onlookers, the scene was one of coffee and cakes, the fragrance of scent and powder, the sounds of English and piano music, numerous soft lights, a taste for expensive installations and layer after layer of misty white cigarette smoke.

Meanwhile, outside the windows the night grew darker, the red neon lights more bewitching, while the autumn winds swept from both sides across the race course facing the hotel.

The journalist Ziyan's report on the fashion show organized by Daisy at the Park Hotel on the 4th of November 1936 reveals some inconsistency. As she saw it, to anyone who did not know where their autumn clothing would come from, the luxurious Tsingyi fashion show was discouraging. But Daisy grew up in the midst of plenty. She knew nothing about poverty or the desire for revolution. She just wanted to establish her own career, in this case in fashionable clothing. She wanted to promote recognition of Chinese dress materials, to harmonize Chinese and Western fashions as a contrast to the Shanghai people's disdain for Chinese products. She told the press that clothing in Shanghai was grotesque and gaudy, and that Chinese products should not be looked down upon. She believed that Chinese silk could compete with English wool, that Chinese women's clothing could be both suitable, and beautiful. In fact, this same line was followed by the Wing On Company in its attempts to spread China's market in the world and build up Chinese industry. But the noises made at the luxurious Park Hotel were too weak. No one believed what Daisy said at the time in English.

Today however, the press reports about the Tsingyi fashion show would be considered highly acceptable. By using the terminology of fashion in describing the national characteristics, they pointed to an elegance that would display the eastern beauty of the veiled figure.

When Daisy first arrived in China from Australia, she thought it

"French Town" is the popular name of the concession inhabited by one-half per cent French subjects, five per cent comprising some fifty different nationalities and a modest "rest" of a million Chinese. The French Concession started life at about the same time as the International Settlement. It is administered by the French Consul General as ex-officio Chairman of the Council with the assistance of an advisory body, of which half is French and the other half foreign and Chinese in equal numbers.

The Council of the French Concession may at first sight seem to resemble in authority and functions the Municipal Council of the International Settlement. The two administrations, however, are of very different types. The provisions of the French reserve the real power of the government to the Consul General, while the Municipal Council is an executive body exercising general control.

A scene of the business section of Avenue Joffre in the 1930s, the delight of many women in Shanghai. Daisy enjoyed sauntering along this street in the weak afternoon sunshine. The narrow footpaths were lined with European-style displays of leather and fur goods. There were tantalizing whiffs of Egyptian cigarettes, French scents, freshly-baked Russian bread straight from the oven and piroshki.

very strange when she saw from the docks in Hong Kong how her elder sisters were wearing silk. She thought these clothes were not for young people. She herself was wearing an Australian skirt made of velvet. But by 1935 she was advertising the new silk fashions created by the Tsingyi Salon in the North China Daily News. She looked upon herself as a most befitting Chinese woman.

These two years of the fashion salon were the most fulfilling period in Daisy's whole life. She had a happy and comfortable home, a flowering love relationship, a beautiful reception room. She was a beautiful young matron; all her childhood dreams had been fulfilled. Furthermore, she was a modern woman with her own career. It was the first demonstration of her determination to lead an independent life in keeping with her ideals, and not simply to be a woman serving her husband's profession. But all this was missed by the journalist Ziyan in the warm atmosphere of the Park Hotel, where Daisy appeared to be a hothouse flower. But from 1958 onwards, Daisy's life followed a tortuous course. During the last 24 hours of her life she looked once more at her photos. With her fingers gnarled by physical labor, she selected one showing her making a tape recording for her students, and said:

"When I die I would like this photo to be my memorial photo because it shows me working."

But back in 1936, war, betrayal, calamities and a host of daily occurrences had not yet touched her. Others saw her life through the eyes of a Hollywood film. Her face was covered in smiles and vitality. Even the shadow between her eyes was beautiful. Her elder sister was occupied with the latest model of imported American cars, her elder brother liked dancing. Everyone said if Fourth Daughter was playing with new clothes in the Park Hotel, as long as it made her happy, then it was all right.

Chapter Twelve

1944
Thirty-five Years Old

What Happened to Her Smile?

Pregnancy takes away the mystery and treasure of a young girl's body. It also diminishes her self-confidence. Her body is no longer tender after carrying a baby.

Daisy and her son, Zhongzheng, on his first birthday.

A photo of Daisy eight years later reveals the smile of a mature woman, conscious and polite, like it veils long days, disappointment and yearning. Already thirty-five years old, she had reached the age of realizing how a gentle smile can cover emotions. It is the smile of a mature woman. In fact it is not a smile, but the expression of imperceptible pain, reticence, self-respect, tenacity. Whatever she did not wish to discuss she concealed with a smile.

Gone was her joyous smile of 1936. But she still held her head high. It was always like that. Sometimes, as I looked at the photos of this young mother, I wondered exactly when that smile at the Park Hotel actually disappeared.

Could it have been 1937 when the Japanese spread the flames of war to the International Settlement? In August, Japanese planes strafed Nanjing Road. Helen left Shanghai for America to escape the war and the Tsingyi Fashion Salon closed. Daisy lost the work that she liked. She became pregnant and decided to move to Hong Kong. But she did not like Hong Kong and returned to Shanghai before the birth of her child. The Japanese bombed her husband's dairy factory and YH became unemployed.

Life was no longer perfect. Gradually Daisy's bitter journey began. But Daisy had no idea of what lay ahead of her. War had taken away the life she liked, pregnancy had deprived her of the mystery and treasure of her body, she had lost her self-confidence. Regardless of how childbirth is hailed as life-giving, it took away her womanly dignity. Was it this year when her smile disappeared? Or was it in 1941? By then her first child, Jingshu, was already three. She wore a bow of ribbon in her hair, a beautiful little girl wearing dresses trimmed with lace. She remembered her father had no job at the time but went out every day. Her mother worked for the advertising department of the Chinese Medical Association journal. She mainly dealt with the German business community. Sometimes she took Jingshu with her in the car to the Bayer factory. When Jingshu was small, some of her toys came from the Bayer Pharmaceutical Factory.

But this was not the same as working in the Tsingyi Fashion Salon. Daisy wanted to supplement the family income although this was not then a necessity. None of their servants were dismissed. Daisy herself

In 1941 the Pacific war began with British and French troops entering the tree-lined streets of the International Settlement and French Concession, along with their tanks and other military vehicles. Just as Shanghai's economy was developing full steam ahead, the city was plunged into war. The dream of a golden future was smashed.

wanted to work. According to the nattering of the Chinese social set in Shanghai, it just showed that the arrogant Fourth Daughter of the Kwok family had married the wrong man. Now she was compelled to show her face in public. Daisy was not upset by what they said. She did not think it was shameful for a woman to work outside her home. It was better than being a parasite. To be able to do something for herself was worth bragging about. Twenty years later she was sent to the Qingpu Reform through Labor Farm to dig fish ponds. No one believed she would be able to withstand the work. But she fulfilled all the quotas set. She came home and told her children there was nothing she could not do. Nor was she afraid of anything.

However, her work with the medical journal did not last. With the outbreak of the Pacific War, the International Settlement was disbanded. Daisy did not want to work for the Japanese and again stayed at home. It was the second time that she had to give up work she liked doing. Now at last she realized what she really wanted was to be able to lead a creative and independent life. But she had not found the means to do so.

Was this when Daisy lost her smile? Or was it in 1939, the year her husband no longer earned enough money to pay the rent? Daisy solved the problem by taking the whole family to live in her mother's house. This must have been the year she lost all hope in her husband. He was always thinking of getting rich quick. Moving from one occupation to another, he had no desire to build up a profession for himself. As he tired of one toy, he turned to another. He was a playboy. He had no sense of responsibility for the care of his family. Feeling that his ability fell short of what was needed, he turned to taking risks. He started a winery and it failed. A partnership in business failed. He found life in 1943 too bitter to face. Zhongzheng was born in October that year and Daisy suffered a difficult birth. But instead of waiting in

the hospital he went off to seek some night life. He probably still loved her but he could not face up to the duties of a husband and father.

I do not know if Daisy reacted as most women did, holding on to the vision of the man she loved as a knight in white armour, asking herself how she could disbelieve one who stood up and pulled out a chair for her at mealtimes, who opened the door for her whenever they went out together, or if there was only one seat on the dance floor would give up his own seat and stand beside her? Yet when she was giving birth to his son, he went off to his club to play cards.

Little by little, the transparency of Daisy's still beautiful face became lost. The smile she now wore was that of an adult woman, like the powder base women used in the 1940s. Like the photos of most women in this position, the chubby faces of their babies smiled innocently as they nestled securely in their mothers' arms.

Chapter Thirteen

1945
Thirty-six Years Old

Easy Come, Easy Go

After the second world war, Daisy and a few friends invited an émigré White Russian chef, who had formerly worked in the Russian Czarist household, to teach them Russian cakemaking. From then on she no longer bought cakes from the local western bakeries.

*W*ith the explosion of the atomic bomb in 1945, the Second World War ended. The Kuomintang government, receivers of the enemy's surrender, arrived in Shanghai and YH discovered that a distant cousin of his, Liu Gong-yun, was the Minister of Finance. He arranged for YH to be given a job with the Custodian of Enemy Property and YH was placed in charge of German assets in Shanghai. Thus twenty years after his return to China, the hapless Woo Yu-hsiang's luck changed. He and his colleagues furthermore regarded the German war reparations as their own property. At last YH's dream of "getting rich quick" was realized and the Woo family prospered.

The following are the childhood impressions of Luo-lun (named Roland in English), YH's nephew.

Third Aunt's family furniture was all the same color, made of Fuzhou padauk and polished till it shone. There were cupboards of silverware and cut glass. The sofas were large and soft; sitting in them was like falling into the clouds. Third Aunt's Christmas tree reached to the ceiling. Her cook made the choicest Fuzhou dishes while the ice-cream made by her was smothered in crushed walnuts.

Third Uncle and Aunt used to go dancing at the Canidrome. When they came home they said they saw the film stars Butterfly Wu and Hsu Lai dancing there.

My cousin had a bow on her head and looked just like a western doll. Her small brother was a chubby little thing. He was always singing nursery rhymes like: "lai" means come and "chu" is go, "nongge" father, that is me.

One day Yu-Hsiang went home with a set of European toys rarely seen in Shanghai. They were toy war models, including many life-like models of soldiers, cannons, airplanes, rifles, flags, all made of good plastic. Each soldier was the size of half a finger and even the buttons on their uniforms were visible. This set had been confiscated from the home of a German. Zhongzheng was allowed to play with this set of finely made toys. He liked them and so they kept them.

Woo had a zest for life. The post-war period was a very happy time for this bachelor of engineering from the Massachusetts Institute of Technology. He was able to provide his family with warm and interesting times. Daisy no longer went out to work, so she and a few friends asked a White Russian émigré chef from the Czarist house-

Daisy, the housewife, with a penchant for security and responsibility and a good life.

The popular Canidrome ballroom where expatriates of all nationalities spent their evenings. Some of the musicians came from Jamaica.

hold to teach them Russian cake-making. After that Daisy no longer bought cakes from the western bakeries. Forty years later, during the 1980s, when her former cook fell and broke his leg, and had to lie in his attic with no one to assist him, Daisy made the same Russian-style cakes at home and rode the bus to take them to him.

The Woos kept a handsome German dog in their home. At family reunions right up to the time of the memorial service for her, somebody would always enquire about the dog.

Now she lived the unworried life of a happy young matron. The children were older and she decided to send her attractive little daughter to classes conducted by a White Russian teacher of ballet dancing. During this period, Daisy used to accompany her husband to play mahjong all night. The Woo family's chairs at the table had no cushions, but Daisy could play throughout the night without having to lean backwards.

Twenty years later, however, the toy soldiers were confiscated a second time, when the Woos were driven out of their home. Which boy's hands were they swept into; whose father took them home? Nobody knows.

Zhongzheng said when the toy soldiers were confiscated he still remembered the day his father came home with them. Watching from the side, Daisy had remarked:

"Easy come, easy go!"

Woo was a temperamental man who carried on in his own reckless way. In 1919, with no understanding of the meaning of revolution, he took part in the student demonstrations in Peking, was arrested and put in jail. In 1945 as an official of a victorious country, he was put in charge of receiving enemy property. But he never regarded these long-resident German merchants in China as the enemy. He took home the toy soldiers of the enemy's child to his own child. He treated the German merchants well and made friends with them. After they returned to Germany they commenced trading with him. As a result he became the owner of his own company.

When the People's Republic was set up in 1949, his business was doing well and his family was in comfortable circumstances. While members of his own extended family began leaving the mainland, he said:

"When the Japanese were here, the people in Shanghai still lived a good life. There is nothing to fear from the communists."

In 1956 Woo's company became a joint-state-privately-owned enterprise. The Wing On Company did the same. During the celebrations of the shift from private to joint-state-private ownership, the manager of the Wing On Company stayed at home singing from the Cantonese Opera *Shandong Xiangma (Shandong Bandit)*. But Woo joined his staff, who were parading on the streets clanging cymbals and beating drums.

In 1956 Woo was sent to take part in a study course at a political school set up for those in industrial and commercial circles. When called on to speak out against what they regarded as shortcomings of the communist party, Woo responded and was named a rightist. As a result, he lost his position as manager and was reduced to the rank of a worker. He went home and told his family he had been asked to wash the floor but he didn't even know how to wring out a mop.

That was in 1957. The next year he was arrested in his office. Daisy received an anonymous phone call, informing her that the Woo family car had been left in Jiujiang Road. By then all the capitalists had locked up their cars in their garages and switched to riding in pedicabs to work. They had also started wearing Sun Yat-sen suits. Woo was the only one who persisted in driving his car till his last free day. When Daisy found their black Ford in Jiujiang Road and tried to start it, she discovered it was undriveable. This led her to conclude that YH was hoping for an accident to take place.

Finally, in 1963, a sentence was handed down on Woo requiring repayment to the state of a huge sum in U.S. dollars and another in *renminbi*. All his property was confiscated as well as Daisy's jewelry and clothing, including her wedding dress and veil which were already falling to pieces. Also confiscated were numerous photos taken by the Skvirsky studio at their wedding.

Chapter Fourteen

1946
Thirty-seven Years Old

Pollyanna

Pollyanna would always say: "I have never believed that we ought to deny discomfort and pain and evil, I have merely thought that it is far better to greet the unknown with a cheer."

*I*n 1946 nobody knew what was going to happen. But the Woo family situation had improved and the children were growing up. So they started going on trips.

To my surprise, I found that Jingshu and Zhongzheng grew up very close to their mother. I thought educated mothers would not be on such good terms with their children, especially a beautiful mother. They told me that when they were children their mother did not take care of their meals or put them to bed. That was the work of their carers. But Daisy had majored in child psychology at Yenching University and when the situation arose she taught them a great deal. She told them many stories and the children had a great respect for her. They cared about her. Even when Jingshu was 61 and Zhongzheng 56, they still argued over which of them their mother liked better.

Both enjoyed a rich childhood. Daisy often read to them from the well-known 20th century American children's classic, Pollyanna. According to the English language dictionaries, "Pollyanna" had become a pseudonym for blind optimism. Realizing that everything had a positive side, she always looked on the bright side and happily accepted whatever she thought was of value to her. She did not care for money. Instead she liked natural and simple things. She always said:

I do not believe we should turn away from suffering, wickedness or hurt, I only think, first of all happily accept the unknown future. That will be better.

Perhaps this was the book Daisy liked best during her own childhood days in the library at McTyeire School for Girls. It was a bestseller in the United States in the twenties. But that was the time when Daisy always held her head up high and ignored others. Why then did she like this book so much?

With the return to peaceful days in 1946, there was no way of telling what value Pollyanna's example would be to this beautiful mother and children.

Both Jingshu and Zhongzheng remembered their mother saying that Pollyanna was indomitable. Nothing could destroy her. But why when she read to her children before they went to sleep did she speak about Pollyanna?

Had Daisy known she would embark on a long and arduous journey during the 1950s, I think she would have moved overseas with other members of the Kwok family. This journey had already begun for Daisy when the ballet ensemble was sent on a performance tour abroad. But Jingshu and others of similar undesirable backgrounds were excluded. It was only through a relaxation in 1962 of the strict policies enforced towards intellectuals that Zhongzheng was admitted to Tongji University. However, he was later placed under house arrest there as a reactionary student. It was at such times that they remembered the bedtime stories their mother read to them about Pollyanna. Thus that happy American child became their spiritual guide.

When Daisy and Zhongzheng were driven out of their home during the Cultural Revolution in December 1966, they were allocated a small six-square-meter room above a kitchen. They had to share a toilet with two other families in the same house. After they moved the few pieces of furniture they were allowed to take with them, they discovered that the roof leaked. Zhongzheng observed a ray of light shining from the roof on to the floor. Fortunately, friends found them some old pieces of plastic and helped them cover the hole. Then one day Zhongzheng said jokingly:

"I think we ought to cut out a few stars and paste them on the plastic. That way I can imagine I am sleeping under the stars."

Recalling this episode in her memoirs, Daisy wrote: "I'm glad he could manage such a cheerful outlook on the whole thing."

Jingshu, Zhongzheng and I talked a lot about Daisy after her death in the autumn of 1998. That was when they discovered they knew nothing about the horrors Daisy had endured She never told them about the labor reform farm during the Cultural Revolution or her feelings when her husband died in the prison hospital. All these experiences she kept to herself. Once she accidentally mentioned to Jingshu that while she was at the Chongming Island Farm she went with the work team to reclaim river mud. According to Jingshu, Daisy said: "I've always been curious. But I was already 60 and physically I hadn't the strength to go down to the river to dig up the mud. So I was given the job of taking care of the boiler providing drinking water. The fire in the stove was never very good. I had to watch it and add fuel. Suddenly it went out so I stuck my head inside to see what the matter was. Just then a draught came down the stove-pipe and the wood burst into flames. My face was covered in black soot, and the hair on half my head, as well as my eyelashes, was burned."

"She wasn't complaining", sixty-year old Jingshu explained. "She was exultant. She was trying to say, you see, I did all those things. I am capable. Earlier she told me that when she was sent to sell salted duck eggs outside the French Park, she learned how to pick out which would yield oil when cooked. We had just been driven out of our home. We had no idea what other calamity would hit us next. But she never bowed her head. She would say that the other capitalists might claim she wouldn't be able to stand it. But she was just like Pollyanna," sixty-year old Jingshu said.

Daisy was not only their mother. She was their mentor.

Zhongzheng said: "The dictionary explanation about Pollyanna is not correct. Daisy's optimism was far more powerful than blind optimism. Just look at my mother and you will understand."

A photo of the three of them taken on a trip to Hangzhou in 1946 shows a beautiful woman in a floral patterned gown, an exquisite little girl wearing an unbuttoned cashmere sweater, and a chubby and peaceful-looking little boy. The three of them shared stories about Pollyanna before they went to sleep. I rejoice that in their good times they had already read about and liked Pollyanna. Just as the sun shone on their faces in the photo taken in Hangzhou, it was Pollyanna who lit up their hearts.

Chapter Fifteen

1948
Thirty-nine Years Old

Elegant Lady's Dark Side of the Moon

From now on Daisy's life became embroiled in eruptions. Like a nut being smashed open, her soul and spirit emitted a fragrance which normal life had concealed. Since then, her life became one that was aesthetic. Others saw magnificence in it, yet she herself emdured endless suffering.

Zhongzheng's pet goat

$\mathcal{B}$y 1948, the year before the establishment of the People's Republic, Jingshu had already done a year's training at a private dance school in Shanghai conducted by a former White Russian ballerina. A number of other children, who in later years became New China's outstanding ballet dancers, were also trained by this Russian teacher. The dance school was a beautiful part of this bold and assured little girl's early days.

Daisy adored her chubby little son, Zhongzheng. Of a natural and gentle disposition, he loved small animals, he was the friend of the family dog and their little goat. He would sob at the top of his voice if he fell over. When he was happy he would chuckle loudly. Like the smallest child in all families, he followed his sister around. While she did not particularly like this she did not begrudge his presence.

In 1947 Y. H. Woo finally started his own company, the Xing Hua Scientific Instruments Company, importing medical equipment. The German merchants he had dealt with while he worked in the enemy property administration bureau had already returned home. Woo had established good relations with them and they started doing business with him. After losing a dairy farm and a winery, at last he was standing on his own feet. By 1948 he had become a stable trader in the international market. With his hair combed back, his face had relaxed while the love of play and fashion of his youth had gradually mellowed with middle-age.

Daisy had developed into a mature and still beautiful woman. She was at peace, but her face revealed signs of past stress. Only an inner strength enabled her not to betray the dignity of the family that she carried on her shoulders. She was the one responsible for this family appearing as attractive as it was. She was no longer the nervous young bride serving the first breakfast. The household staff included a young house boy named Songlin who waited on the table, a maid called Jin Hua and a master cook from Fuzhou. Songlin frequently broke the bowls through careless handling and Jin Hua would complain to Daisy. Fifty years later Songlin said:

"The young mistress asked Jin Hua how the porcelain shops would be able to survive if all the bowls were unbreakable. But later, when no one else was around, she said:

"Next time don't carry so many bowls. Just be more careful."

The Woo family was acclaimed by all, including children, for its warmth, westernized life-style and harmony.

"That was what she was like," Songlin said.

He was present when she died fifty-one years later on an autumn evening and wiped away her last tears.

There is no doubt that Daisy was the core of her family. This is revealed in a group photo taken in 1948. By covering her face with your hand, this perfect family looks as if it had slipped its moorings. Jingshu on Daisy's right appears ill at ease. On her left, Y. H. Woo's face carries a suggestion of sadness, not visible before, like a flame approaching extinction. Take your hand away and Daisy is again in charge of them all. They are still a family envied by others.

But if you cover up the faces of the children, there is no sign of the joy Daisy and Y.H shared in their engagement photo taken on the stone steps in the garden of the Kwok family home. Something has been added instead, something like an agreement between business partners. There is a hint of distance and disagreement, like the well-known expression of a settled husband-and-wife relationship. That is, of course, after the dust has settled on extraordinary occurrences.

But by 1948 Daisy's life was peaceful and calm, as in other families after more than 10 years. By looking backwards one could see the years ahead. Perhaps her children would grow up like this, her husband would gradually become older, more responsible, like the greeting cards in 1948 with their wishes for "peace in years to come." Life would go on like this until someone died of old age; there were no more complaints.

Had it been like this, however, Daisy would have remained an uncracked walnut. No one would ever have known what kind of a heart and spirit was concealed inside that hard shell.

I first saw photos of Daisy forty years after this one was taken, in the home of a photographer friend. That was when I saw two photos of Daisy being made into lantern slides. One was Daisy's engagement photo. The other was taken more recently of her on the same stone steps. The black hair of the young woman had become white. The man standing by her side was not to be seen. That was also the first time I vaguely heard her story. It was about a girl from a rich family who suffered in a red city. Such stories were not unique. I remembered it but was not particularly moved.

Then a few years later a friend from Singapore asked me if I would go with her to visit an elderly lady, a very interesting person. Although she had suffered enormously, she had left China 6 times but had still returned 6 times. My friend had met her in Singapore and heard her say that one night she dreamed the Cultural Revolution had returned. She asked herself if she would be able to stand it again. She decided she could still go through it once more. My friend laughed and said:

"Don't you think this old lady is fun? After going through so much, it seems she didn't care. This is really unimaginable to us people overseas."

So I went along with her. It was very cold that day. Daisy stood before a small round table and pushed an old-fashioned quartz heater towards me, saying:

"Warm yourself up. It's very cold today."

This was the elderly Daisy. Her hair was as white as snow. She was wearing a sky-blue sweater and looked a picture of beauty. Talking about herself, she said:

"If there had been no Liberation, no Anti-Rightist Movement, no Four Clean-Ups Movement, no Cultural Revolution, I wouldn't have suffered. But then I would never have known how much hardship I could take, how much strength I had. Now I can say that as a result of all my experiences I have lived a very rich life."

The Liberation took away her life-style; the Anti-Rightist movement took away her husband; the Four-Clean-Ups Movement took away her normal life; and the Cultural Revolution took her house and property as well as her family. So from 1966 she had to start living on her own.

Looking at this photo again I recalled the first time I had heard Daisy speak. It was very dull and cold that day. There was no central heating in the room. This photo drew a fine line through Daisy's life. Before the line she had lived a soft and easy life, like a hamburger. It was from here onwards that her life became shaken by waves of hatred. Like a nut being smashed open, her soul and spirit emitted a fragrance that normal life had concealed. Since then, her life became one that was aesthetic. Others saw magnificence in it, yet she herself emdured endless suffering.

"If I had not remained in Shanghai I would be like the other members of my family who went to America. I would have lived the life of a young lady of the Kwok family. I would never have known that there was nothing to be afraid of, that I could face anything," Daisy said.

At the age of 88, Daisy was living alone in the winter in an unheated room, but her smile of pride shone like diamonds. From the time of our first meeting, she had fascinated me. The smile on her face was rarely to be seen on an elderly person. It was full of vitality, pride and charm, indomitability and wit. It was the kind of innocent smile only seen on a child's face. I long to see her smile again. Her face was like fish in a pond at night, splashing out of the water, their glowing bodies flashing by in the dark. I feel her presence but I cannot see her. How I wish I could see her again!

Daisy told the story of her life at 88 as though she rejoiced that she had never lived a peaceful or drab life. During the last year I spent with her, she showed me an album of photos published in New Zealand. All the photos were of old people. She said:

"Only when one is really old, is it no fun. You can't do anything then."

This was the only complaint I ever heard her make. She went on, saying:

"Look at the skin on their faces, how loose it is. Their smiles are covered in wrinkles. It doesn't look nice."

Sometimes happiness in a long life can be dull, but who would lift their own hands to destroy their own happiness. The long and rich life recorded in the photographs left us by Daisy is now over. If Daisy had held on to keeping the family together to the end it would have been a waste of her talents. If it had not been for the last 50 years those qualities would never have been released. The people of the world would never have known the fragrance of her heart, perhaps even herself included. Very often I had not the heart to press her further about the calamities she had faced. Repeating everything was like going through it all again, she had told me.

The memoirs that Daisy left for her family she wrote up to the 1970s, and then stopped. She admitted she had not finished. But she did not have the courage to go on. Was it because after the calm in the 1970s there were no events to stimulate further writing? She had hardly described the privileged part of her life. Nor had she said much about the quiet period after surviving the downward trend. In fact it was the hard times that she felt so disinclined to talk about that had transformed her into an outstanding daughter from a rich family.

Chapter Sixteen

1951
Forty-two Years Old

Too Naive to Foresee
the Future

During the early 1950s Daisy and YH often traveled back and forth between Shanghai and Hong Kong. They never felt any urge to leave Shanghai for good. Like the vast majority of the Chinese people, they saw the fifties as the beginning of a golden age.

$\mathcal{F}$ollowing the setting up of the Hsing Hua Scientific Instruments Company, Daisy began accompanying her husband on business trips to Hong Kong. The three years from 1951 did indeed turn out to be a golden age for Shanghai's national capitalists. The chaos of the civil war and the uncertainty of where to go before 1949 was at last ended. Shanghai's capitalists breathed a sigh of relief under the newly raised red flag and began to live a peaceful life. The dust had settled. There was no more war, no more roving soldiers, no more racketeering. So long as they exerted themselves, there was every promise of great progress to come. Even playboys like Woo Yu-hsiang were filled with pride and threw themselves into developing their business enterprises.

In Hong Kong Daisy and YH came across people they had known in Shanghai who now found themselves in a quandary. During the 1950s, this southern peninsula known as Hong Kong was more like a small country town compared to Shanghai. Suddenly it was swarming with well-educated people speaking the Shanghai dialect who were used to a refind way of life. They expected to be able to continue their businesses in the same way they had in Shanghai. But they found the Hong Kong market was undeveloped and controlled by gauze-jacketed and wooden clog-wearing Chaozhou traders. The new arrivals from Shanghai faced crushing defeat. After their last gold bars were spent, the only way their modern young daughters could help their families out was by working as dance hostesses. Their princeling sons had to sell the new American cars they had just bought. In these circumstances, the majority of Daisy's Kwok family relatives decided to migrate across the Pacific to America.

Their observations convinced Daisy and YH they had made the right choice. They congratulated themselves for neither panicking nor

In 1951 Daisy's well-off friends remaining in Shanghai took it in turn to host weekend gatherings at each others' homes. This photo shows the relaxed atmosphere in which they lived at the time.

destroying their lives through their own actions. Together with most of the capitalists who chose to remain in China, they applauded the arrival of the new society.

They and their remaining friends in Shanghai resumed their weekend parties at each others' homes. Having evaded the Japanese during the war and the Kuomintang after the war, they emerged from their places of hiding. One of Daisy's photos taken in 1951 by her younger brother, George, is a reminder of those days. On that particular day after a sumptuous luncheon prepared by the host family's chef, the men had sat back and chatted. The women had talked about the flower arrangement classes they had been attending after discovering them in the advertising pages of the evening paper. The children had scampered about in the garden until late afternoon when the parents called them together for this group memento.

In years to come Daisy had to use a magnifying glass to see how tall her son had grown by then and how long her daughter's plaits were. But she could no longer place the year when this particular photo was taken, whether it belonged to the pre-Liberation period or to the early 1950s. As she remembered it, there was very little difference between the years of those two periods. The Kuomintang's flag with its blue sky and white sun had been replaced by the Communist Party's five-starred red flag. They hardly paid any attention to the differences between these two flags.

During their frequent visits to Hong Kong, it never occurred to Daisy and YH to consider not returning to Shanghai. They shared the widespread conviction of others that the 1950s were a golden age. What did it matter, they thought, when one day their application to go to Hong Kong again was not approved. They simply went on with their daily lives and work as before.

Chapter Seventeen

1954
Forty-five Years Old

Career Woman Again

*I*n 1954 tighter state control was introduced over the conduct of foreign trade. From then on English was the only foreign language allowed to be used in commercial correspondence. The Hsing Hua Scientific Instruments Company was trading with Germany and until then its correspondence had been handled by a German secretary.

The company's German secretary returned to Germany and the firm's business correspondence was then written in English by the employees and sent to Daisy to be corrected. As time passed, Daisy became formally installed as the company's English secretary.

This was her third professional job and she was paid a monthly salary of 200 yuan in the national currency called *renminbi*.

Chapter Eighteen

1955
Forty-six Years Old

Daisy Starts Wearing Slacks

The first time I saw a photo of Daisy wearing slacks, an odd feeling came over me. The photo reminded me of a girl I once saw in a beautiful pair of Japanese silk stockings over which she wore a pair of white sneakers!

But by 1955 people like Daisy gradually became dubbed as relics of the past. They began to be careful. It was no longer considered suitable to wear cheongsam or long gowns so Daisy started shortening her long gowns into blouses.

$\mathcal{A}$s we went through Daisy's photos of the various periods in her life, she often found it difficult to remember where they had been taken, who had taken them and when. She would say:

"Look at what I am wearing. If it is western clothes then I still hadn't graduated from McTyeire. If I am in slacks and a top altered from a long gown, then it would be after the mid-fifties." So I chose a photo of her in a top cut down from a long gown taken on a vacation with her lanky son. Jingshu had already gone to Peking to attend the ballet school there and eventually became one of China's first generation of ballerinas. An odd feeling came over me at this first glimpse of Daisy in slacks. The photo reminded me of a girl I once saw in a pair of beautiful Japanese silk stockings over which she wore a pair of sneakers!

In 1955 the Hsing Hua Scientific Instruments Company became a joint state-private enterprise. The top managerial staff voluntarily reduced their salaries. Y. H.Woo led the way by cutting his monthly pay from 600 to 300 yuan. Daisy also offered to have her pay cut to 148 yuan.

Chapter Nineteen

1955
Forty-six Years Old

Leading a Double Life

From the age of forty onwards, Daisy's experiences began enriching her mind. This could be seen in the gradual modification of her features, the wrinkles on her face, the look in her eyes, the way she smiled and the shape of her lips.

A spring outing at Mogan Hill, a resort near Hangzhou. Why did they choose to be photographed on a collection of rocks?

$\mathcal{T}$he photos taken in 1955 reveal the dual existence Daisy had begun living. One, taken on an outing with their colleagues, shows Daisy and YH wearing simple baggy cotton garments, referred to as people's clothing. Their crumpled simplicity suggests they still felt out of place. But when Christmas came round, they dressed as meticulously as before in their own home. Daisy would wear a pair of American nylon stockings, which she had saved. All this reflected a lack of confidence and self assurance, that they had something to hide. They no longer

felt bold. Thinking back, Daisy told me in 1995 she thought their secret was that they had put up a Christmas tree instead of a portrait of
Chairman Mao, and she had worn nylon stockings and a long gown
instead of people's clothing.

*While we were both working in the foreign trade corporation, we used to go
to a coffee shop after lunch. It was usually crowded at lunch time. A stranger (to
me) motioned that we could join his table. We did. Then I realized YH knew him.
He handed YH a package wrapped in newspaper, which YH dropped into my bag.
When we left, he told me to give it to him after work when we got home. I insisted
on knowing what the contents were and he said he had done some business with this
man, and this cash was his share of the profits.*

*From time to time YH would ask me to meet this man (Mr. S, who was Jewish)
and get a package from him. I suspected something wasn't quite right, but followed
instructions. One time I was told to go to the Park Hotel's new restaurant in the
penthouse and have lunch with this man. I was a bundle of nerves and could
hardly eat. After I had received the package I couldn't get away fast enough.*

*After YH's arrest I received a phone call from this man to meet him at a certain
place after dark. I went, roamed up and down the street at the appointed place but
did not see him. Suddenly he appeared out of a doorway, took my arm and said,
"Let's go to a nearby restaurant. I'm afraid this spot is being watched." (When I
look back, I guess I must have had pretty strong nerves). I followed him and he
gave me the package. He told me he knew YH had been arrested and this was the
last package. I never saw him again.*

*One day some time later, while I was at the office, security asked me to go to a
separate room as they wished to ask me a few questions. They laid out 7 or 8 passport
size pictures and asked me if I recognized any one. I immediately recognized Mr. S,
but I picked up each picture and gazed at them one by one and shook my head.*

*"All foreigners look alike to me," I told them. "I can't distinguish one from the
other."*

They told me to take my time and look carefully. My brain was twirling around trying to decide what to do. Then one of them said to the other,

"It's already noon, let's continue after lunch."

They told me to go and have my lunch and return afterwards.

When I got back, the pictures were laid out on the table again in a row. I glanced at them and then noticed a sheath of papers on the table beside them. I recognized the handwriting. It was YH's. Pretending to be looking at the pictures I read what I could on the written statement. I noticed the name Mr. S and after it I read the words (translated) "only my wife knows about this." I realized YH had confessed.

I looked again at the pictures, appearing to concentrate very hard, and then said,

"I really can't tell, but this one seems a bit familiar."

I picked up Mr. S's picture.

"What is his name?" they wanted to know.

I told them I couldn't remember names, but they told me to think again, so I said I thought it began with an S.

"Yes, that's right, now tell us all you know about him."

So I told them the story of how I met him at the coffee shop, and that I understood he was in business with my husband, and how sometimes my husband had asked me to receive a package for him, but I never knew what the contents were. They were satisfied with my report and told me I could leave.

Before the age of forty, a woman's looks are inborn. Whatever beauty she has comes from her family and her good fortune. After forty it is the kind of life she leads that develops her mind. From then on changes take place in her appearance, on her face, in her eyes, in the shadows between her smiles, in the shape of her mouth. Many people say that after a woman is forty, the kind of life she has led can be read on her face, whether or not she is beautiful, what her outlook

The drawn curtains and closed windows create an atmosphere of trying to retain the limited temperature. Such photos suggested a snowman in the sun as it gradually melted into a pool of water.

is, how warm her heart is, what drives her spirit. But Daisy's photos showed no great changes. While there were more lines on her face, she seemed to be more patient, more emotional, more lively and flexible. There was also a hint of the modesty and courtesy practiced by members of capitalist families as a result of the double life that had been imposed on them at the end of the 50s, enabling sensitive people to easily distinguish them from ordinary people.

Yet in spite of all this, by the nineties and after forty years of leading a double life, Daisy's face, her curls and lipstick, still expressed the gentle charm and aesthetic standards of a traditional woman. I envisioned a crafty fox at the edge of a dark forest, white snow covering the ground, questioning her opponent's intentions, ready to escape, the forthrightness and sincerity of her twenties all gone.

Zhongzheng arrived from America, just before the start of the memorial service for Daisy in 1998. He had shared Daisy's calamitous period from the time he was 14. As he looked up at the low ceiling where his mother's portrait was surrounded by chrysanthemums and lilies. Mozart's *Requiem* was about to be played, this solemn chorus taking the place of the *Funeral March*. The musician was testing the sounds while Mozart was being played intermittently. The fragrance of thousands of freshly cut flowers permeated the atmosphere.

Zhongzheng stood with his hands by his side as in his childhood photos, gazing at the photo of his mother. Her fox-like spirit was clearly discernible from her photo. His red eyes were filled with tears. I thought of the words of the French composer Marguerite Duras: "I love even more your devastated face." Zhongzheng knew best the changes that had taken place in his mother's face, how much grief was contained in her love.

Chapter Twenty

1957
Forty-nine Years Old

Beside a Decorative Garden Rock

In 1956 Daisy's husband dug a hole under a decorative garden rock and hid the third revolver in it. That was the third Pistol that they had taken care of for George.

Taken in 1957, this is the last photo showing Daisy wearing a long gown and a full smile on her face.

*W*ith the approach of 1957, Daisy's family was still living under the pressure of a double life. When her daughter, Jingshu, came home from Peking, they used the family camera to take photos in their little garden. They put on ostentatious long gowns, which they no longer dared to wear outside their home and snapped one photo after another, under the trees, by the flower beds and sitting on the grass.

Jingshu laughed as they continued shooting scenes of the decorative rocks before the flower beds. She was a frank and open young girl.

Life seldom cast shadows on her mind. She frequently reminded her little brother of the western-style courtesies towards girls when they went out together, such as opening doors for them, helping them on with their coats, paying for the coffee, walking on the outside in the street. Whenever Zhongzheng forgot, she would gently tap him with her foot, but she did not nag. Furthermore, she was quick at grasping a situation for what it was. In explaining the searching and sealing of their home, she raised her hands and said:

"No problem. We still managed. They took away all our cutlery. So we went to the Seventh Heaven Building (an extension of the Wing On Department Store) to the apartment-homes of the Kwok family upstairs who had already left Shanghai, and helped ourselves to what we needed. So we lacked for nothing."

While the photos were being taken, Daisy sat smiling by Jingshu's side. They were like two fresh flowers. But I imagine Daisy must have had many more worries on her mind than Jingshu. At the time there was a small hole at the bottom of the decorative rock behind them and this was where the third revolver that Daisy's husband had taken care of for her brother, George, was buried.

Before 1949 the Kwok family were threatened with the danger of kidnapping, so the men always carried a revolver. Eighth younger brother George was planning to sneak across the mainland border to Hong Kong, and he worried most about the firearms in his office. The government had forbidden the private holding of firearms and George feared he would get into trouble. He might even be prevented from leaving if he handed them in. So he had asked Daisy to help him dispose of the first two.

Taking the first two revolvers, Daisy and YH set out in their car during the night. They threw one onto a lonely road. The other they took to Pearlie's holiday garden in the Hongqiao area and while no one was looking they dropped it into the creek that flowed through the garden.

However, the day before George planned to leave, he went to clear away the contents of the desk of his second elder brother, Leon who had already left Shanghai. All of a sudden a secret drawer opened up and inside it there was another revolver. George himself was an unsophisticated person and now found himself in a perilous position. He couldn't replace the secret drawer, so he went again to Daisy in the night and asked her to dispose of it. Daisy's husband agreed and Daisy thought they would have to make another night trip. But YH said he had a safer method and would bury this really useless weapon for the time being. Right up to his arrest, however, he never explained what his better method was. When Daisy died forty years later she still did not know what he had intended to do with that useless revolver that had brought so much trouble to the family.

During the earlier years when firearms were easily obtainable, YH had indulged himself with cars, cards, and dancing. He was fascinated by American baseball but he never touched firearms.

Meanwhile George took the train south and went off to the United States via Hong Kong.

One year later in 1957, when Daisy had her photograph taken sitting on top of the revolver George had left behind, she little realized that this would be the last photo with her original smile or that her life was about to undergo a complete change.

"They were so inexperienced," Jingshu commented forty years later. "Fancy leaving the revolver there! Uncle George could have left it in the office. Anyhow he was leaving, he was going to be in America. My parents were so naive. How could they have buried it at home! They could have tossed it anywhere. Who would know it was they who had thrown it away! How could they leave one in the little creek in Auntie Pearlie's garden! When the creek dried up and was cleaned out, everyone saw that revolver. Auntie Pearlie was frightened out of her wits. Luckily my mother never told Auntie Pearlie that it was she who had thrown the revolver there. Auntie Pearlie could never tell a lie and another person would have been incriminated."

Auntie Pearlie was a girlhood friend of Soong Mei Ling. Auntie Pearlie was already terrified at having such a girlhood friend.

After George left, YH took a garden shovel and buried the revolver in the garden. Daisy watched him from the small balcony upstairs facing the garden. He was already more than fifty years old and not very agile. Moreover, he was totally unused to such physical exertion. White shadows reflected his body on the dark bamboo walls of a thatched cottage as he bent over to the crunching noise of the low palms. With the sagging of muscles at the corners of his eyes he looked a picture of misery. Daisy would never forget that night. It was quiet and not too cool, a Shanghai evening suited to secret activity, when a husband and wife aged more than fifty carried out this daring but puerile action.

Chapter Twenty-one

1958
Fifty Years Old

The Longest Day of All

Daisy and her husband never discussed the plight he found himself in. Perhaps Daisy was not as strong-willed as she later became. Perhaps neither wanted to face the shadow hovering over them. Or they preferred to pretend that nothing had happened.

*I*n 1957 Woo Yu-hsiang was named a rightist and Daisy's life of purgatory began. Already the Hsing Hua Scientific Instruments Company had formally become a joint state-private enterprise and subsidiary of the Shanghai Machine Tool Import-Export Company. YH had been appointed chief of production and was dispatched to the Shanghai Industry and Commerce School of Political Studies for a period of study, popularly referred to as "brain washing." While at the school, he responded to the communist party's call to speak his mind. He probably thought the correct thing was to take an active part in any movement sponsored by the party. His own natural disposition was not well established. He was easily excitable and had no particular motive. It was rather like the way in which he took part in the May Fourth demonstrations in earlier days. He further risked being labeled a counter-revolutionary for listening to American broadcasts. It was not because he was interested in the anti-Chinese propaganda or the news from the blockaded western world. He simply wanted to follow the American baseball results.

At the school he made the acquaintance of numerous members of Shanghai's industrial and financial circles. They went on outings and had dinners together. In effect, they became cronies.

It never became clear what YH really thought, either then or later. Neither Daisy nor her two children could tell. They still went on family trips, they ate together, took photos in their garden. But YH suffered from a serious case of asthma. With the changes in the seasons he coughed and sneezed as regularly as the cuckoo in a wooden German clock appearing to announce the time of day. But they never discussed the position he was placed in, or the imminent disaster about to hit them. Probably Daisy was not as strong-willed then as she was to become and they preferred to believe that nothing had

By 1958 Shanghai's streets were more like a little country town. As Daisy drove the family car home in March that year, did she remember that the basic gentleness, which many longed for, was still there beyond the terror?

happened. Talking would only make things worse. So as the shadow moved closer, they buried their heads in the sand.

In 1957 YH came across his name in a list of rightists published by the *Jiefang Daily*. What he did not know, however, was that nothing in his personal file indicated that he was a rightist. In fact in 1980, when the cases of all the rightists were re-examined and overturned, YH had died twenty years earlier in the Tilanqiao Prison Hospital. There was no evidence that he had ever been declared a rightist. Therefore he could neither be nor was there any need for him to be rehabilitated. No one appeared to know how his name came to be included in the list of rightists published by the *Jiefang Daily*.

At the time, however, YH was quickly removed from his post as production chief and made a cleaner. He went home and asked the servants to show him how to wring a mop dry. He had never done any such work before. Now at last Daisy and YH realized that instead of getting the chance to build the fortune, they had lost everything.

Daisy too was sent to a study class for capitalists and left her office in the building along Shanghai's city riverfront, known as the Bund. For the first time in her life, she learned how to wield a heavy hammer to break up large stones into chips for road construction. She also learned the necessity to wear thick gloves.

On the 15th March,1958, Daisy was told to return home as the police were waiting there to see her. Ever since their maid had stolen some U.S. dollars from them, no policeman had entered their home. This was the second time. She found two policemen waiting for her. They told her that YH had been arrested. They asked her to put together some clothes, bedding, towels and toilet paper for his use and take them to the Sinan Road detention centre, which had a reputation for housing serious criminals. But no toothpaste or toothbrush was allowed in case the toothpaste contained poison or the handle of the toothbrush might be used to commit suicide.

"I almost collapsed when the policemen said this," Daisy said.

Just then she suddenly heard strains of music coming from the piano in the downstairs sitting room. Someone was playing the same tune that Zhongzheng had been practicing that week. She quickly realized that her 14-year old son, Zhongzheng, had returned from school. Normally he never liked playing the piano. Nor did his parents entertain the hope that he might become a musician. They simply wanted him to learn something about music. Daisy wondered at Zhongzheng's enthusiasm for the piano that day. But the sound of the music comforted her. Her son was home. Only a third year student in middle school, he was still her son and the thought calmed her.

Thirty-seven years later Zhongzheng returned to Shanghai from America to see his mother. He said he still remembered that day on 15th March. It was a day he could never forget. That was the day he became an adult. Until then he was only a boy interested in playing. On the first day of each school term, Daisy would call him to her bedroom and ask him to pay attention to a list of do's and don'ts. By the beginning of the next term she would repeat these instructions.

But that particular day when Zhongzheng returned home, he was stopped by their cook who seized hold of him and warned him that something serious had happened. Two policemen were upstairs with his mother. Zhongzheng decided he wanted his mother to know he had returned. He couldn't very well go upstairs. So he went to the piano in the sitting-room. The cook rushed at him, waving his hands in alarm and tried to pull Zhongzheng off the piano stool.

Zhongzheng said: "But this way mummy will know I've come back ..."

Daisy said the music restored her senses. After the policemen's

The black sedan shaded by a tree at the back was the little Ford of the 1930's left standing in Jiujiang Road.

visit, they packed up the things YH needed to take to the detention centre.

Before they had time to leave however, the telephone rang. A strange male voice told Daisy that the black Ford YH had driven to work was parked on Jiujiang Road, not far from his office. Then the phone was hung up.

Zhongzheng and Daisy set out for an address in a very busy city street. They had to walk along a grey wall to the side opening of an iron gate where they entered a low building. Inside was a long wooden counter, behind which sat policemen not wearing their caps. Daisy and Zhongzheng were given a number. Thus in one evening, Daisy's husband and Zhongzheng's father became a number. Up till his death he was known as No. 1675.

While the policemen examined the things they had brought for YH, Zhongzheng stole a look through the door. He saw a low pine tree in an empty yard. It seemed quiet and peaceful, which surprised the fourteen-year old. This was the memory he retained of the view from the gatehouse where his father was now living. For the next three years, it was Zhongzheng who came here instead of his mother, she being unable to come, to deliver whatever his father needed. Each time he waited until the policeman who took the things away returned to the gatehouse with a receipt signed by his father with his number. His father's acknowledgment indicated that he was still alive. Not only was the receipt proof of contact. It comforted the now fatherless boy.

Every time Zhongzheng went to the jail, YH requested that he bring some cotton thread. It was not until after YH's death when Zhongzheng and Daisy went together to receive YH's belongings that the mystery was solved. They discovered that all the buttons had been cut off his clothes. In order to fasten his clothing YH had rolled

萦萱妻，中正兒：

我現在已移到南車站路192号第一看守所，我身体很好，勿需掛念。

我現在需要：依夫肝油丸，維他命片，不仗油葡萄糖鈣片，及棉毛衫褲（內）二条，卒內衣兩套（褲子仍用褥子和鬆緊帶，不需帶子）衣褲拖鞋各一双，布毛巾兩塊，盆浴白條

以後每月的接濟你们于照所内規則每月送 柴品等等物件你们也可以自动用邮包寄，但是小菜不需送了，另外你们可以存点錢在管理处入我的賬，以便随时買些需需的東西

胡葉耀 3/22日

This statement, or his last words, was addressed to his family by Woo Yu-Hsiang one week after his arrest. For the first time he addressed Zhongzheng as though he were an adult. It signified to Zhongzheng that his father was handing over to him many family responsibilities, including the care of his mother. Written in 1958, the statement was kept by Daisy during several house removals until her death in 1998. It is one of the family heirlooms which Zhongzheng took to America for safe-keeping.

the cotton thread into little strings to take the place of buttons. Neither of them had ever seen the once elegant and talented YH using cotton strings instead of buttons to fasten his clothes. The last time he left home he was dressed in a simple cotton people's suit in the same neat way that he used to wear western suits.

This was certainly the longest day in the lives of Daisy and Zhongzheng. After delivering the bedding and clothing they went to Jiujiang Road near the Bund to drive their car home. The black Ford was already very old. When the private business companies became joint state-private enterprises the capitalists who worked near the Bund curbed their airs and began travelling to work by pedicab. Or, like their employees, they went to and fro by bus. YH was the only one who continued to drive his car to work and then went straight to the toilets to do his cleaning. The Ford had not been kept in good condition after the amalgamation of the private enterprises. But by then it had become too ostentatious to continue travelling in one's own car. Daisy had urged YH not to drive the car any more but he would not listen to her. However, he no longer allowed her to ride in the car and made her take the bus instead.

Daisy and Zhongzheng found the Ford parked by itself in the darkness of Jiujiang Road. Without a single tree and lined on both sides by tall buildings, the street had a cavernous appearance. They got in the car but when Daisy tried to start it she found it in very bad shape. Every now and then she almost lost control.

They turned into Nanjing Road and shortly afterwards reached the Wing On Department Store ablaze with lights. Built up by Daisy's clansmen, from the time she had left Australia and come to China, it had provided her with a healthy and wealthy life for fifty years. But this was no longer to be the case as the back of their car receded further and further away. They drove past the Park Hotel where during the 1920s Daisy had burst into the photographer's shop and taken down her photo from the display window. YH had then stolen the photo and hung it in his room. For Daisy the Park Hotel signified the establishment of the Tsingyi Fashion Salon in 1936; it had been the venue of the family's Christmas party every year; it was also where she met the mysterious Mr. "S" who handed her a packet of money. It had about it the air of Manhattan of the 1930s. But Daisy had no thought for all this that night. Perhaps if the car had been in better condition she might have recalled the story written by the journalist Ziyan, in which she movingly compared the gap between the poor and the rich young ladies who had attended the Tsingyi Fashion Salon's fashion show. Did Daisy imagine that her life too would be overtaken by such a gap?

They drove down Yan'an Road to close by the old Kwok family residence with the big garden. Whenever Daisy faced difficulties in the past she would go home to her brothers and sisters, her powerful father and mother. The children in this family were then unaware of any matters beyond their control. But now they were spread over America, their parents were dead and their old home belonged to the state. No longer could Daisy do as she did in the past when her leg was injured in Hangzhou, driving home to ask her brothers to bandage it. Probably she had no time that night to dwell on sentimentality. Terrified of an accident, she turned again and went home.

She revealed her thoughts from that night in her memoirs with one sentence:

As I drove home in this car, which never should have been driven, I thought YH must have known it was already undriveable, and he was hoping for an accident.

If I thought my husband was hiding such despair I would be stricken with grief. I wonder if Daisy was like that. She said very little about this, nor did she say anything to Zhongzheng who was with her all the time. After returning home she carefully parked the car in the garage and never touched it again until it was confiscated by the government.

On their return, they found the Woo house was as quiet as it had been the day before. The palm tree standing near the hillock where the revolver had been buried continued its crunching in the breeze. As the weather grew warmer, the path where YH used to park his car on his return home from work emitted the smell of leaked gasoline. But from then on life changed for everyone as far as the Woo garden was concerned.

Taken in a park in 1958. (left to right: Daisy, Pearlie, her husband and Zhongzheng).

Zhongzheng called Daisy from behind as they entered the door, saying:

"Mummy, I grew up today."

It is my guess that one of the photos was taken towards the end of 1958 just as Daisy's family began getting used to the reality that a member of the family had become a number. Pearlie and her family were the only close relatives remaining in Shanghai. This photo was taken when they all visited a park together to lighten their spirits.

Daisy is shown, still smiling, but her smile lacks expression. It does not reflect the unswerving lack of fear or evil she was later to develop. She appears distracted, absent-minded, even forgetful. In 1958 she had not yet adjusted to her new life. She still did not know what was best to do. She had begun wearing slacks while Pearlie still wore a coat and skirt. A second life had started for fifty-year old Daisy, a completely different life that was full of theatrical contrasts. If ever she had felt defeated, this was the moment.

This was one of the worst photos taken of Daisy in her whole life. It shows her neck sunken in her collar. Her smile is resentful, her old delicacy is no longer visible, and the sparkle in her eyes was yet to come. For the first time in a photo her hands are not ceremoniously placed before her knees. This was because her study class was taking part in the nationwide drive to make steel. They had built a simple homemade smelter in the garden of a house in Changshu Road. They had removed the iron railings, iron gate, including the old-fashioned lock which they were smelting down in the midst of boiling black smoke. Daisy's hands were rough and covered in cuts and bruises. In this photo she resembles more a silkworm painfully showing its head as it sheds its skin.

On the other hand, Daisy's sister Pearlie smiles elegantly as she sits closely by her well-known pediatrician husband. The two sisters were the only members of their family who remained in Shanghai. While Pearlie's situation was clearly deteriorating, Daisy's misfortunes served as a warning to her to be vigilant for her own happiness. Was it because she felt more fortunate or that she relied more on her husband? By covering up Daisy on the left and Zhongzheng on the right, they present the unusual view of a mature couple sharing a tender and mutual dependence. It is in the misfortunes of those close to us that we often find proof of our own security and happiness. This is what makes people feel grateful and compassionate.

Zhongzheng looks seriously into the camera. He must have thought it unseemly for a mature boy to smile. Certainly not like the photos showing his father relaxed and at ease. Thin and tall, he appears totally unlike the chubby little boy of 1946. From the day he announced to Daisy that he had grown up, he shared responsibility with her for all matters in the family, including secrets.

Pearlie's husband is shown smiling at the camera, one hand round his wife, the other on his nephew. He was also a Tsing Hua University scholarship student sent to the United States. With the arrest of his fellow student and in-law, his outstretched hand shows the responsibility he feels for the care and comfort of this now fatherless boy. The photo reflects both his warm-heartedness and concern. This was only to be expected as he was the one remaining man within the Kwok family.

This fleeting picture presents a contrast between grief and happiness. I could not help feeling a deep sorrow after picking it up.

It was too real, too cruel a blow to Daisy's dignity and pride.

If you look at the photo long enough, you can almost hear the crushing of the walnut. You share Daisy's pain. Only then is the fragrance of the pale yellow nut released.

Chapter Twenty-two

1958
Fifty Years Old

The Smile on Her Swollen Face

In the midst of this sublime state, a time of violence was coming closer and closer, like a large iron pot approaching boiling point. Slowly but surely, the pot became hot, then red hot, and eventually boiled over.

*A*lthough the public mood was optimistic, step by step an age of madness was approaching. Like a pot of water put on to boil, it was heating up. It was a long and quiet process, but eventually the water would reach boiling point.

Because her family was in trouble, Jingshu, already a member of the Central Ballet Troupe in Peking, took the opportunity afforded by a slack period to return to Shanghai. She found the family living as quietly as before. Her brother had grown taller and because he was interested in photography his mother had given him a camera. Very few boys had a camera in those days. They were expensive. At school he had been abused for a long time over his given name of Zhong-zheng. This happened to be the same as one of the names that Chiang Kai-shek, who had fled to Taiwan, had chosen for himself. It was widely assumed that Zhongzheng, with his family background, was named after the generalissimo. The truth was that when Zhongzheng was born, his father had pondered over his own school days and the difficulty he had in brushing the many strokes in the characters form-ing his name. He wanted to give his son a name with fewer strokes. In the end, Zhongzheng himself altered his name by adopting oth-er characters with the same pronunciation but a different meaning. Originally, his given name meant the centre, now it meant loyal to the government.

Jingshu noticed that apart from the absence of her father, the family's houseboy, Songlin, was also missing. A sincere lad from a family living along the coast, he used to take her to and from her ballet classes. He also took Zhongzheng out. He took care of the children when their parents were not there. At times he was like a playmate. He had left the Woo family to work in a factory. Little did they realize that one autumn day fifty years on Songlin was the one who would stand in for them when Daisy passed away. It was Songlin who brought back her last memento, the fringe of her white hair braided into the figure of 90, her age when she died. This represented a salute by the Chinese Red Cross Society for donating her remains to medical research.

Daisy seemed to be as happy as ever. Jingshu asked about her mother's new job. Following YH's arrest, Daisy was told by her office, which was situated on the Bund, that her work would be changed. She was sent to the foreign trade department's farm at Zhengben Road in Jiangwan district in the northeast of Shanghai. There she was given the job of feeding the pigs. Jingshu became very interested in the rearing of a piglet. She discovered her mother was equally interested. She told Jingshu that when she was in Sydney she used to feed the family's two ponies. She liked the ponies so much that when she had to leave Sydney she experienced for the first time what it was like to be broken-hearted. One of the ponies was called Dolly, the other was Nick.

Daisy took Jingshu to the shops below the Jin Jiang Hotel to have an overcoat and suit made. This was where Shanghai's most exclusive tailoring establishment was located. It had old-style polished wooden counters and was well lit. The air was suspended with the fragrance of woolen fabrics and scents that could be encountered no where else. While inside this shop Jingshu thought her mother looked as beautiful as before.

Daisy then took Jingshu to a beauty parlor. They discussed a new hairdo for her and Jingshu returned home transformed. Zhongzheng made her pose for photos of her new look.

After Daisy went to work at the farm, Zhongzheng, adding to the little lamb he had cared for when he was small, acquired a chicken which Daisy bought at the farm.

Zhongzheng could not remember the lamb he had cared for. He hardly remembered the lovable German dog the Woo family had. But he could never forget the little chicken, which joined them after the peace of their garden became disturbed towards the end of the 1950s.

Because he was still fairly young, the farm agreed she could return home every day, unlike the capitalists there who were undergoing reform through labor. But Daisy had to wait until after political study was ended in the evening. By the time she arrived home Zhongzheng was usually asleep.

She had to get up at five o'clock in the morning to hurry back to the farm, returning home after ten o'clock at night. This involved crossing from one side of Shanghai to the other. Sometimes she was so tired that she would fall asleep on the bus. One night she found a seat and just as she was about to doze off, she was woken up by the person next to her. He had fallen asleep and leant his head on her back. Daisy turned his head around, but very soon he leant on her again. Then she turned her head in the other direction. By the time the bus had taken them past dim lights and sleepy streets, Daisy too was asleep. When she woke up there was only a ticket collector waiting for her. She had arrived at the bus terminus, a place she had never been to before.

Stepping off the bus, she found she was lost. She waited for a long time trying to work out where to go or see passers-by. She did not telephone her home, nor to Pearlie to ask her husband to help her just as many years ago he went with Daisy to the young widow's home to fetch her husband home.

I cannot understand why she didn't look for a policeman to help her. In those days if a woman lost her way at night, she would first look for a safe place where she could ask reliable people for help. The police station with its red light would be the safest. In those days the people relied on the police, they regarded the police as heroes, the protectors of the weak. All the children used to sing:

"I found one fen by the side of the road and I handed it over to the hand of uncle policeman."

Most people felt no threat at that time. They were leading active but simple lives. They saw themselves as good people, living in a happy era. But in fact, there were already those like Daisy, who felt stripped of all power.

In the midst of this sublime state, a time of violence was coming closer and closer, like a large iron pot approaching boiling point. Slowly but surely, the pot became hot, then red hot, and eventually boiled over. While the surface water still appeared calm and far from boiling, those unfortunate drops at the bottom of the pot were already scorching hot. Fate had placed Daisy and others at the bottom of the

pot. They were the first to bear the brunt of what was coming.

Daisy could not remember how many residential districts she walked through that night. Finally she found herself in a place she knew and at last arrived home.

Zhongzheng, like all growing children, was sleeping soundly. With only the time of a dark night allowed her, Daisy woke him up. This was the one time she woke Zhongzheng up when she got home in the middle of the night. He opened his eyes and saw Daisy's smiling face as she opened an old squashed cardboard box. Inside it was a tiny baby chick looking like a ball of wool. Daisy placed the box in front of Zhongzheng. From then on he had a real pet, a White Wyandote chicken! Both Zhongzheng and Daisy loved the baby chick. It had not long been hatched when Daisy brought it home. By the time it grew to the size of a dove, Zhongzheng photographed it. He became very upset when later on a weasel killed it. Together they dug a grave in their garden for it. It was while they were digging the grave that Zhongzheng noticed Daisy's hair had started going grey.

The photographs clearly showed Daisy's hair was turning white. Although her general appearance was like that of any woman dressed in cotton clothing, the upright way in which she stood, straight as a ramrod, suggested she had great poise in her younger days. This was the beginning of Daisy's world of difficulties. She wanted to put up a smile to cover up everything, which gave her face a swollen look. Maybe this coincided with the menopause. I think it must have been the early 60's when Woo Yu-hsiang's death laid all these problems to rest. Daisy had no time, like other women, to pay attention to the physical changes that normally occupied the major attention in a woman's life. To Daisy they were no problem at all. Her swollen smile covered up the life she was experiencing. The days when she would spread her hands over her lap as she had in 1958 had passed. But she

In 1958 Daisy's hair began turning grey.

In 1958 Daisy's slightly swollen smile was said to resemble someone whose face had been trodden on.

began to discover an inner strength. Perhaps it was the self-respect she always had which ensured the smile on her face.

Now Daisy placed her hands behind her back to hide the changes in her fingers. During the winter months she was sent to work in the godowns at the foreign trade wharves for frozen exports, stripping the outer leaves of the wongbok cabbages brought down to Shanghai from northeast China.

The cabbages were cold and damp. She had to work on them all day, removing the spoiled outer leaves to ready them for export to Hong Kong. Many of her family members were still living there. Hong Kong was George's destination when he left Shanghai. It was the last place Daisy and her husband had visited across the border.

By the time Daisy finished her work every day her hands were frozen stiff. From then on her fingers began to stiffen and she was no longer able to do fine work. She said:

"Thank goodness I didn't feel much pain. It's just that my fingers were no longer flexible."

In spite of all this, Daisy thrust her chest out and strode forward as though, like all women, she wanted to cover up the thickening of her waist. However, I noticed that her body was becoming more lax, despite the broadening of the hips that older women have. These changes were as clear as the signposts along the highways.

During 1958 the farm was extended and Daisy spent most of her time fetching and carrying cement for the construction workers, mixing the cement and climbing up the bamboo scaffolding to deliver buckets of it, a dangerous and tiring job. When Jingshu asked about her mother's work, Daisy said:

"Look! I can climb so high. The capitalists say they are not afraid of hardship, nor even of dying. What they fear is falling down and not dying. But I am not afraid of anything!"

Thirty years later Daisy met Jacqueline Kennedy, the widow of former U.S. President John F. Kennedy. When she asked Daisy about her reform through labor, Daisy said:

"The physical work enabled me to keep my figure and prevented me from putting on weight."

Another photo of Daisy at this time showed the walls of the Woo family garden behind her and the palm trees at the end of the wall. This was where the police dug a hole and found the revolver confessed to by Woo Yu-hsiang, rusted beyond use.

The police came a second time a few days after Woo's arrest to question Daisy. They carried out a minute search of the Woo family home. She had to open up all the locked places and display all the family assets. These were then sealed, including the hiding places for jewelry, gold bars and American dollars, all of which Woo had told them about.

Daisy weighed up how, without harming her husband nor refraining from telling what he had already disclosed, she could avoid harming herself. She feigned an inadequate knowledge of Chinese so as to gain the extra time it took to translate from Chinese into English and thus enable her to consider what she could say, what she must say. When the police spoke in Chinese questioning her, she pretended ignorance and asked what they wanted to know.

I thought of her play-acting at McTyeire School for Girls, the photo of her on a garden bench discussing affairs of the heart with another young girl, a fellow student in the part of a suitor. Those experiences were being put into practice!

The police asked Daisy: "Have you hidden anything you should not have?"

Her reply: "I don't know what we should not have."

Police: "Illegal things."

Daisy: "I don't know what things are not allowed by law. Can you give me an example?"

Policeman: "Well, like guns, that sort of thing."

Then Daisy understood. So she said: "I think we have a gun here."

Policeman: "Do you know where it is?"

Daisy replied: "In the garden. Do you want to see it?"

She then gave them a shovel. The same one that Woo had used to bury the gun and went with them to the decorative stone in the garden by the side of a tree.

After the police found the revolver and a box of cartridges, Daisy wrote out a statement for them. This was the reality of Daisy's life that the photos revealed. If Jingshu and Zhongzheng had never asked they would never have known, but once they did they saw the situation in the same positive light as Daisy. They also saw an always active mother, one whose heart was not so easily crushed, never lacking in love or determination.

Daisy told them clearly about their father. She said:

"Your father wasn't without fault. He did many immoral things, for example, taking the money from the Jewish man."

This enabled them to understand what was really just, and the need to establish the truth on the basis of facts, not covering up evil with evil.

I grew up in the chaos of the Cultural Revolution with the simple and placid mind of a child. But I can recall many horrible sights and stories. I always thought a person should not experience too many difficulties or hardships, just as a clean sheet of white paper cannot stand up to too many erasures. Eventually a sheet of white paper will no longer look clean, while a person who suffers too much will become resentful.

Listening to Daisy, I felt shocked. My childhood years had passed so fleetingly and before my eyes I was witnessing a marvel. Was it a result of Daisy's natural disposition or was it the bright and airy library at McTyeire or did all this take place during the quiet whitening of Daisy's hair? This was when I discovered my own fragility and pessimism. I was so happy to find someone at last whose story contradicted the theory of the formation of pessimism in early childhood.

I became euphoric in telling my friends about it in a flood of tears. Like fire which turns sand into gold and reduces paper to ashes, I saw behind Daisy's faintly swollen smile the purity of spirit of a little girl flashing its light.

Chapter Twenty-three

1961
Fifty-three Years Old

Scene from the Balcony

Even when her own choice did not bring her the happiness she expected, she stuck to it, cherishing whatever joy it did give her. Nor did she evaluate others on the basis of her own gain.

$\mathcal{H}$ad it not been for Zhongzheng's obsession with photography I don't think Daisy would have kept the photo of herself on the balcony of the Woo home. Her husband had died a week earlier and she was still wearing a black jacket. She is shown standing in the same place where she stood one night in 1956 watching her husband bury the third revolver George had brought them, when the concealment of weapons by private individuals was prohibited as a counter-revolutionary crime.

Perhaps Daisy was unaware she was about to be photographed. Taking advantage of the light, she was waiting for Zhongzheng to focus his camera. But what she saw was the heap of fresh soil under the tree left by the policemen after they had dug up the revolver. Her thoughts gravitated to the one who had buried the gun. He would never return now.

The look on Daisy's face brought back to me the treasure chest we had at home when I was small. It was made for our family by a master cabinet maker and was used by my two elder brothers who were building crystal radio receiving sets. The chest contained resin, sticks of tin, electronic tubes, electric wire, all sorts of spare parts, and was fashioned out of unpainted boards nailed together and divided into numerous compartments. When the lid was shut it looked like a big wooden building block from a kindergarten. I liked those blocks in kindergarten but I hated going there. I often sat on our treasure chest and let my imagination roam freely. Although the chest resembled a big block, I knew it contained all sorts of treasures.

Without moving or saying anything, the expression on Daisy's face in the photo suggested she was seeing the freshly dug up soil below the verandah while her son quietly snapped her. I thought of what might be going on inside her.

Shouldn't there be a compartment for pain?

On the 2nd December, 1961, Daisy was notified by the jail that her husband had died in the Tilanqiao Prison Hospital of heart and lung complications. She was to be allowed to view his body for the last time before the cremation. When Daisy asked why she had not been notified to visit him before he died, she was told "your whereabouts were uncertain."

"What a lie!" Daisy exclaimed to me.

During the three years of his confinement she or Zhongzheng had gone each month to the detention centre to deliver the things he needed. Throughout this time Daisy was undergoing reform through labor at the farm. She was not permitted to absent herself for one single day. Zhongzheng had not been accepted by any university after he finished senior middle school because his father was in custody. He was therefore studying by himself at home while Daisy paid one and a half yuan to a private tutor for each of his English lessons.

When autumn came round Daisy went to the detention centre to ask that she be allowed to send her husband some household medicines he had formerly used. But her request was refused. The prison hospital would take care of him, she was told.

Then she asked if Zhongzheng might accompany her on her last visit. The response was:

"The son may come but he must be guaranteed not to make a scene."

Zhongzheng said: "Don't worry, Mummy, naturally I won't make a scene in front of them!"

Daisy and Zhongzheng went together to the Prison Hospital at Tilanqiao. They were taken to the morgue, which was housed in a small room. Daisy was shocked at the sight of the almost flat looking bodies lying on the narrow pallets.

"So thin," she thought to herself in horror. Not having seen her husband for three years, she still had a vision of a tall middle-aged man. He had certainly not put on any weight, but how he could be the thin frame lying there?

She later thought:

"YH's head was like an apple stuck on a chopstick. He looked as though he had starved to death."

There should be another compartment for all the fears.

When she and Zhongzheng decided to go and identify the body, others advised she might not recognize it, in fact it might not be that of her husband. In such a case she should examine the hands. A person's face might be changed beyond recognition but the hands would not show much difference.

Thirty-five years later when I was paying a twilight call on Daisy, we talked about her husband's death. Leaning over the small round table that separated us, she stretched out her hands, already much

Daisy covered the casket containing Woo Yu-hsiang's ashes with white calamas as a symbol of her affection for a simple playboy.

changed in their appearance, and said:

"That was the first time that I learned it was difficult for a person's hands to change. I really could not recognize him. He was such a thin corpse. So I felt his hands, which I knew so well and they were his. Then I knew it was him. But later I thought, hadn't my own hands changed? This shows that a person's hands can change. If I changed places with him and he were to feel my hands, I doubt he would know it was me."

Zhongzheng did not cry. He just felt cold all over. Daisy laid her handkerchief over her husband's face and took Zhongzheng home.

She did not cry either.

A few days later Daisy went and took home her husband's ashes and personal belongings. She had busied herself with the funeral arrangements right up to this time when the ashes were placed on a table. Bending over the standard-sized casket she had bought from the crematorium for the ashes, Daisy said in a choking voice:

"It doesn't matter whether one lives a longer or a shorter life, but three years of your life were wasted."

This was Daisy. She had married YH because she appreciated his zest for life. When his fancies wandered she fetched him home because he was the male head of the family. But self-respect would not allow her to strike him when he was down, nor would she attack the lady of his fancy to revenge his infidelity. She just wanted to say one last thing to him.

Words failed me when I learned that Woo Yu-hsiang had once had an affair. What an insult this was to the pure and honorable Daisy. How could she not be disappointed, fly into a rage, or hate him! He gave her all the happiness he could but he also caused her all the pain she suffered.

I thought of Zhang Ailin and Hu Lancheng.

Daisy never said much about her husband. Even in her memoirs she said very little, with no comment at all. But the one sentence she said over his ashes showed that of all people Daisy was the one who understood Y. H .Woo best, even though she no longer loved him. She understood best Y. H. Woo's foibles, his untutored fascination for new things. Yet despite all she went through, she upheld her own choice and did not repudiate him.

This was the pride and self-esteem that Daisy possessed. She upheld her own choice. She did not discard it because it did not bring her the happiness she expected. She cherished the joy she got from her own choice. Perhaps never lacking for anything herself, she never looked to gain from someone else. She simply adhered to her own inclinations. This persistent pride was displayed by her in the winter of 1961 when she welcomed back her husband's ashes, like a shower of sparks when something under heavy pressure is in motion.

However, this was still not Daisy's darkest period. Even worse awaited her, when her sense of pride would shine like a torch.

We shall see more. Much else was contained in all those compartments, concern, appreciation, pain, despondency, conceit, and stubbornness. But Daisy, with her face always facing the sun, covered everything up. Even her photographer son, Zhongzheng, would not dare to say he really knew about each incident that took place in his mother's life:

"She never spoke about the evil vented on her, never complained."

He said this in 1998 when there was no longer any threat of revenge hanging over the old Daisy. Within the family the next generation wanted to know exactly what Daisy had suffered. But she said very little. Could it be that one of the little compartments contained the pride that was so characteristic of Daisy all her life and was sealed up in its fragrance by transparent resin? The greatest pride of any woman regarded as having been treated unjustly is to remain silent.

All those who have served sentences in jail know the custom not to take anything with them when they are released, to signify that they never want to return. But Daisy took all her husband's personal belongings, including the enamel mug, which she used for many years.

Chapter Twenty-four

1961
Fifty-three Years Old

Christmas Eve

"Within Total Darkness, There Arose A Glorious Light"

That was when I learned that after being driven out of her own home to live in a densely populated city area, Daisy made many St. Petersburg-style cakes in a smoke-blackened wok.

$\mathcal{B}$ecause they came from Australia, the Kwok Bew family kept up the tradition of a family reunion on Christmas eve. While George Kwok Bew was alive, he always presided over this occasion.

While Dadda was alive Christmas was the main event of the year. Every member of the family who was in Shanghai, and their families if they were married, attended. Some close friends were also invited. It was Dad who decided who should be invited. There were so many presents that the dining room table stretched all the way into the parlor. The Great Eastern Hotel (which was part of the Wing On Co.) catered for these luncheons. It was a real western meal with turkey, plum pudding and all the trimmings. That was the one day of the year that Dadda celebrated with the whole family.

After Dad passed away we carried on this family tradition. As the families grew bigger we started having a Santa Claus as well as the Christmas tree. With Santa Claus distributing the gifts the children were so happy and excited. We made it a rule only to give presents to the younger generation, but just to watch their delight made the occasion more festive than ever.

Daisy described all this in her memoirs. While writing about the death of her husband, she suddenly switched to recollecting the family reunions each Christmas eve. There was no transition from one event to the other. She told how as the older members of the family left Shanghai, it finally fell to her to organize the annual Kwok Bew family reunion at the Woo family home. During the early fifties, a photo of the largest Kwok gathering ever was taken, before most of them scattered to the four corners of the world. But by Christmas Eve in 1961, when the remaining members of the clan gathered at the Park Hotel, only two tables needed to be reserved. There was no more hubbub of voices, the remaining faces appeared slightly restless

One of the group photos of the Shanghai Wing On Kwok clan taken at their final gathering in the early 1950s before the majority left China for Australia, Hong Kong, the United States and Singapore. Never again was a gathering like this repeated.

and not altogether at ease.

On this particular Christmas Eve, Daisy wore a black jacket, and with her already graying hair freshly set, went to join the Kwok family, as she had done so many times in the past. It was a totally different Christmas Eve. Her husband had died just 23 days earlier.

I could not help but admire her indomitability. Although she had grown up in a missionary school, she was not overly religious. It was not necessary for her to set aside her personal feelings to fulfill this obligation. They had a simple meal, which enabled those who had little opportunity to see each other to exchange family talk. Daisy was now neither young, nor old, and already a widow at the age of 50. Her only son's future was no longer assured, while her daughter was not allowed to accompany her ballet troupe to perform abroad due to her family background. There was nothing Daisy could do to ease her family's fate. Nevertheless she went to that Christmas Eve reunion and was photographed with the others.

Those attending had no idea at the time of the changes that had taken place within Daisy. Later, when they had more time to think about it, they conceded that it was not easy for her. But at the time they saw no great change. She was as lively as ever and she showed no animosity towards the majority of them who had not dared attend her husband's funeral. But her face in the photo taken reveals her grief, the weariness caused by her work at the farm, her unease at being looked down upon. It suggested the quiet stillness of a small animal caught in a trap, as well as natural resentment. None of this could be covered up. Daisy is shown sitting in the midst of relatives who had stayed on in Shanghai. Boldly tilting her head upwards, she looked graceful and charming, like a sensitive woman posing before the camera. She was the most eye-catching of all.

However, following this Christmas Eve, the situation went from bad to worse. No longer could the Kwok family have another Christmas meal like that. In fact, the Park Hotel stopped serving Christmas dinners. The families of Daisy and Pearlie became the only ones left to spend Christmas together, by which time Daisy was practically destitute. So they would gather at Pearlie's home instead. Daisy only had to make a cake and this is what they did until Pearlie died.

The Christmas after Pearlie had passed away, for old time's sake, I asked

Jeffrey and Ella to have Christmas dinner with Mae and me at the Blue Village Restaurant. The menu was excellent, but as luck would have it Jeffrey had a bad cold and did not attend. The next year when even Jeffrey had gone, I asked Ella to have dinner with us at the same restaurant, and she took her sister along to keep her company. Then Mae left for the States so that was the end of celebrating Christmas for me.

In her memoirs Daisy describes in great detail how she spent each Christmas Eve, writing ten times more than what she wrote about her husband's death. This is how Mae, unhappy at the time, later described the Christmas Eve dinners as her best memories of Shanghai:

We would go to the restaurant and sit down. Nainai (grandmother) would first tell us how to eat dinner, and how to help ourselves to food. She always looked so beautiful and elegant. Even then she attracted much attention. Many of the customers couldn't take their eyes off her, including the restaurant staff. They always assumed she was a foreigner, which at that time was considered a great compliment.

After meeting Daisy in 1996, I frequently dropped in on her just to have a chat. When I returned from the United States in 1995 I brought back some cake mixes. All you had to do was to add eggs, water and heat and even if you didn't know how, you could still make a big cake. I was hoping to be able to entertain my guests with cakes made by myself. But I didn't realize that we did not have an oven, so I left the stuff in a cupboard for a year past the use-by date. Then I threw them out.

When I told Daisy this, she shook her head and said:

"You don't need an oven. The next time you come I'll show you how to steam them in an iron wok and still make delicious cakes."

This was when I learned that after she was driven out of her home,

The first Christmas Eve spent by the now widowed Daisy at the Park Hotel. Under the glare of the lights, did she see a vision of her tall, unrestrained deceased husband's head looking like an apple stuck on a chopstick?

Daisy at a reunion with the Kwok Bew family in the United States in the early 1980s.

she made cakes in a blackened-over iron wok on a coal ball stove. She had made so many Petrograd-style cakes this way. There and then I decided to get to know her better and write the first story about her. It was her infinite sense of determination that moved me. What was it that motivated her to so bravely retain the minutest details of the way of life she was accustomed to? She broke off her engagement to Albert, she advised her elder sister not to take part in the demeaning Miss Shanghai competition, she gave up wearing western clothes, she persevered in the face of all the storms and squalls that confronted her. What brought together all these qualities in her?

Chapter Twenty-five

Summer 1962
Fifty-four Years Old

Golden Toast on a Coal Ball Stove

If ever you don't have a toaster, you must know how to make toast with an iron-wire frame. This is what you really need to know, and learn right now.

*A*fter Premier Chou En-lai made a speech in 1962 in Guangzhou calling for a relaxation of the political restrictions that were being imposed on intellectuals and other citizens, Zhongzheng became accepted as a student by Tongji University.

Thereupon Daisy asked for leave from her farm work and took Zhongzheng to Peking to visit Jingshu. She had not been back since her own graduation from Yenching University in 1934.

It was summer time when pony carts clipped-clopped along the wide roads between the city and countryside. The entrances to Peking's little lanes were piled high with green-skinned water melons, while stall owners would slice open luscious-looking water melons to solicit customers, fanning aside the flies with brown cattail leaf fans. The lotus flowers were in full bloom in the imperial garden ponds, exuding their fragrance in the strong afternoon sun.

Soon after their arrival, Daisy took Zhongzheng and Jingshu on a visit to a quiet courtyard much frequented by her when she was a student. It was the home of her best friend, Luo Yifeng. Luo Yifeng's mother was China's first woman graduate of Columbia University, Kang Tongbi, whose father was Kang Youwei .

Summer in Peking is delightful when you can sit beneath a tree in the hot afternoon sun and listen to the cicadas. You can look into the distance above the north China plain while sipping fragrant jasmine tea. Tiny bits of dried jasmine petals, as thin as a cicada's wings, float on the surface. You can sit like that all day, recalling the past or thinking about nothing.

Daisy had not enjoyed a summer like this for a long time. But then she was young, beautiful and proud. Years afterwards, her fellow students still recalled the haughty young Miss Kwok:

"We all knew about her. She was captain of the tennis team. One of the men students almost went crazy when she broke her engagement to him. He used to wait for her all day in the campus. But she didn't know us. She was so stuck up, coming and going without greeting anyone."

This is how former Yenching students remembered Daisy, even years later.

During her student days, Daisy often went home with Luo Yifeng for the weekend. Both were attractive, fashionable Yenching students of respected family backgrounds. In the mornings they would make toast on an electric American toaster in the kitchen. It only took a minute for the toast to spring out after you switched it on.

One morning Kang Tongbi came into the kitchen and took out a wire-frame. After telling the cook to stoke up the coal-ball fire, she taught the two girls how to place the slices of bread in the wire-frame and toast them over the coal ball stove. She preferred toast made this way and she dexterously turned out toast just like the electric toaster. Placing the toast she had made before the girls, she said:

"If ever you don't have a toaster, you must know how to make toast with a wire -frame. This is what you really need to know and learn right now."

That was how Kang Tongbi taught Luo Yifeng and Daisy to make toast with a wire-frame that morning. But they still went on using a most expensive and fashionable toaster, which was replaced by a new one after it wore out.

Daisy had never told anyone about this before, probably because she did not realize the significance of that morning. Twenty-eight years later when she re-encountered the far-sighted Kang Tongbi, she still had not used a wire-frame toaster. But she had lived through the breaking of her engagement to Albert, while her love for Woo Yu-hsiang had led to an engagement party of 200 tables in the

Swiss-designed garden of the Kwok family's Lucerne Road residence. However, she had had to battle on her own when she gave birth to her son. Then came war, the establishment of the People's Republic, the incident of the gun, and her husband's arrest and death.

After that came the endless cleaning of toilets. In 1958 when she was first sent to a brain-washing class for capitalists, she had to clean the women's toilets before anyone arrived in the morning. The local children followed her about and she had to carry out their instructions until they were satisfied. She not only learned how to clean toilet buckets, but also how to obey orders. Whatever she was told to do, she did. There was no argument. She went on to clean even dirtier toilets in the countryside. There the toilet buckets were placed in pits dug into the ground. Daisy had to extricate the buckets from the pits and deliver their contents to the ponds where they were emptied, then take them down to the river to be washed. From then on she learned to do the dirtiest work on her own. Cleaning the toilets was considered to be a form of punishment as well as demeaning. It was not regarded simply as another form of labor. Those sent to clean the toilets had no one to help them. Nobody sympathized with them. They had to rely on themselves and it was like this every day.

With all this behind her that day in 1962, Daisy could not help recalling the morning Kang Tongbi taught her to make toast on a wire-frame over a coal ball stove. Outwardly calm, the two women embraced and enquired about each other, but it was an emotional meeting.

Jingshu was living in Peking and often went to the Kang home where Kang Tongbi also taught her to make toast on a wire-frame. This time the now elderly lady accompanied Daisy and her two children to the Summer Palace. They took photographs by the side of the lotus-filled imperial lake. Although the black and white photo Daisy

Taken with Kang Tongbi in the cool summer of 1962 by a lotus pond in one of the imperial gardens.

showed me was old, the very sight of it evoked the fierce heat of the north China sunshine, and the lotus flowers, the green lake water and the fragrant green grass by the side of the lake, cool and thick, strong and comforting.

Daisy told me all this 34 years afterwards, in 1996. On the same day she said she would teach me how to make delicious cakes using an iron wok over a coal ball stove.

She said: "Of course, steamed cakes aren't exactly like baked ones, but if you can control the temperature, they may not be quite as fragrant, but they will still be very tasty."

But I didn't feel like making cakes that day, probably in the same way that Daisy felt in the 1930s, when she failed to follow up with the use of a wire-frame toaster. So I said:

"Let's wait till I get some more cake mixes from America."

Daisy said: "We don't need cake mix. We can use even better recipes than the cake mix.

But she didn't persist. Nor did I. How foolish I was!

Chapter Twenty-six

Summer 1962
Fifty-four Years Old

Rowing with Both Oars

Daisy never spoke of her grief to her children or complained about her husband. She restrained herself to conceal the sorrow she felt at being widowed in mid-life. This is the pain a mother endures out of love for and to protect her children.

A song extolling the splendors of Beihai Park became well-known during the 1950s. It created beautiful memories of those years, fostering the concept of having reached an age of peace that was to last until the early sixties. This was an era of activity, hard work, honesty and even romance. The numerous visitors to Beihai Park would sit in little hired boats on the lake, gazing at the ripples of green water while their hearts responded to the melody of the song:

Let us row with both oars
While the little boat pushes aside the waves
In the reflection of the White Dagoba.
Surrounded by green trees and red walls,
The little boat floats in the middle of the water
As a cool breeze blows towards us.

While I was pouring over the photos of Daisy and her family taken at the Summer Palace that day in 1962, I wondered if they had ever heard about or thought of this song. Both the summer palace and Beihai are former imperial parks. One of the photos showed Jingshu's smiling young face lit up by the sunshine. She was wearing the dress Daisy had made for her at the Jin Jiang Dress Salon and reflected the very spirit of that song.

Besides photographing his smiling sister, Zhongzheng had managed to catch the high clouds floating in Peking's blue skies. Visistors from the misty city of Shanghai never fail to be moved by Peking's white clouds. When I was 16, I returned to my birthplace of Peking for the first time. Seeing the white summer clouds floating elegantly in the sky, I wanted to cry. Only songs could describe them. I don't know if Zhongzheng felt the same way. There must have been a

Boating on a green-colored lake in the summer of 1962 while inhaling the fragrance of the timber of a sun-dried wooden boat.

breeze when Zhongzheng caught Daisy's and Jingshu's faces with the white clouds in the background. Daisy's arm is outstretched to catch the breeze. They spent as happy a summer as was possible that year. Daisy knew that her just fatherless daughter would not be allowed to go abroad to perform. As for Zhongzheng, he had almost missed the chance to go to university. But Daisy never said a word against her husband, quietly accepting her widowhood, in order to conceal from her children the pain she suffered.

Sitting behind the happy looking Jingshu, one of the photos shows Daisy facing the water-borne breeze. Her face is relaxed, like an icicle melting in the sunlight. Might she have thought of this children's song? Perhaps she would think the song was too gentle, but it was undeniably beautiful. She was after all someone who had made toast over a coal stove with a wire toaster and enjoyed it.

The next year, in 1963, Daisy was sent away from Shanghai to be reformed through labor in Qingpu County. It was the first time she really left home. She had no idea what would happen or when she might return. All those sent there were targets of reform and they were housed in former duck sheds:

This is how Daisy described Qingpu in her memoirs:

Straw was laid on the damp ground and our bedding was laid on top of it. In the morning the straw was damp and we had to carry it outside to dry it as best we could. There were 8 of us in this small shack and we were so cramped that we could hardly turn over at night without disturbing the person sleeping beside us.

Our make-shift dormitory was by a stream. When I asked where I was to get water to wash my face and brush my teeth, I was told to get water from the creek as the country folk did. I carried my wash basin to the bank of the stream and looked down. People were washing clothes, others were washing vegetables, but what shocked me was to see further up the stream some were washing their wooden commodes. For 3 days I just refused to wash, I was told that even our drinking water came from that same stream, but alum was put in to purify it.

As Daisy later recalled, she spent her first hard days at Qingpu digging fish ponds. However, shortly after her arrival she received a summons to return to Shanghai and report to the Public Security Bureau. She took a boat back. Before leaving, her fellow reformed citizens advised her to quietly let Pearlie know in advance the direction she was going to follow so that she would not disappear. She got ready to leave, and also mentally prepared herself against the possibility of arrest.

She traveled by a wooden junk along a river of green water. There was also sunshine, but the southern sun did not penetrate the dense green river water, which was said to be infested with fatal parasites. Daisy sat over her luggage, which rode on top of a cargo of coal cinders. The little junk wound its way through lush green fields of yellow flowers of towel gourd, purple milk vetch, wild white chrysanthemums and pink morning glories. She spotted a little girl from a peasant family, skipping and running along the river bank, picking flowers and sticking them in her hair.

The sight of this unnamed river in the suburbs of Shanghai comforted Daisy as she made her way back to Shanghai in 1963 at the summons of the Public Security Bureau.

After her arrival in Shanghai, a policeman in the uniform of the court handed Daisy a copy of the verdict reached on her husband, Woo Yu-hsiang. He was sentenced as an active counter-revolutionary for having engaged in illegal foreign exchange dealings by selling his foreign exchange holdings in Hong Kong to foreign traders in Shanghai for national currency. He had further offered bargaining concessions for greater sums, regarded as detrimental to the state's interest. In his home he had concealed a revolver in a sinister plot. Daisy was therefore ordered to repay on her husband's behalf US $64,000 and 130,000 yuan in *renminbi*, the national currency.

Another house search took place as well as the drawing up of a thorough settlement. The three diamond rings given her by her father were valued as equivalent to 300 yuan. The household linen and porcelain dining sets for guests were also given estimated values and taken away. After the confiscation of all the family assets, Daisy was informed she still had to repay on behalf of her husband 140,000 yuan in national currency.

Daisy was not arrested but she became the debtor responsible for repaying her husband's debts.

Her memory of that return trip to Shanghai remained with her for the rest of her life. Shortly before she died she still mentioned the quiet little river, which she never could find again. The countryside was so lush, so quiet, so wonderful, she said. Then there was the little girl in ragged clothes, her head covered with flowers, showing how happy she was.

I went to see Daisy on the afternoon of the 24th September in the autumn of 1998, taking along some fresh roses. It was less than 24 hours before she died. I had tried to make an appointment with her over the telephone several times before this. She could no longer eat, felt very tired, and said:

"I only have to make the slightest effort and I have to lie down. I just throw myself on top of my bed."

Her old houseboy, Songlin, was already taking care of her. Jingshu had left two weeks earlier but was worried about Daisy's health, so Songlin put off his daughter's marriage in order to take care of Daisy. Only then did Jingshu leave.

It was during this period that one day Daisy suddenly felt like having some small wonton that were being sold by a street vendor. She sent Songlin out to buy her one serving. But Songlin said what was sold on the street was unhygienic. He would make her some instead. Daisy sighed and said:

"I stopped being a young mistress long ago."

But Songlin persisted. By the time his wonton were ready however, Daisy had already lost her appetite.

When Daisy saw the roses she chided me for spending so much on them. I assured her they were not expensive, that flowers in the autumn couldn't be expensive. Besides, autumn roses had a beauty of their own and would soon be over. I placed the roses in her hands, which felt very cold. She hugged them and smilingly said:

"They are really beautiful!"

She was so weak she could not lift the vase and for the first time asked me to help her fill it with fresh water. Then she put the roses in the vase and arranged their stems and leaves. She re-arranged the buds below that were just beginning to open and said:

"I have always loved flowers, throughout my whole life."

I rejoiced within myself for taking the flowers. It was the last time I witnessed her fine beauty breaking into a smile. I thought of the ring, which I had bought at the entrance to a church in the old city of Warsaw. The silver ring was shaped like a rose. I do not know what controls their opening or withering.

Chapter Twenty-seven

1964
Fifty-six Years Old

The Pot Boils Over

Dark passions mingled with criticism burst out like the explosion of sewerage pipes, comparable at times to volcanic eruptions.

$\mathcal{T}$he stories circulated by Daisy's friends attributed her sufferings to the Cultural Revolution. Perhaps that was how we got used to thinking about it. My own impression was that until 1966 the situation was fine, that the good days lasted up to the summer of 1966 when they suddenly ended like the turning off of a tap. With the help of Zhongzheng, I managed to sort out Daisy's papers before she died and I found that in her case it was not like that at all. In fact, during the 1950s the pot was placed on the stove and it was already heating up, passing from lukewarm to scalding. Most people were not aware of this. Not until 1966 when the pot boiled over, and the situation got to totally out of control, did they become alarmed.

But Daisy's tribulations began much earlier. Hostility was already searing her, and by the time the Four Clean-Ups Movement started, the cruelty dealt out to her had reached the height of madness.

When Daisy turned 55 in 1963, she should have been entitled to retire. Instead she was transferred back from the farm to the office and made a typist. She thought this was the prelude to retirement. But very soon she was sent to the Foreign Trade Department's Spare-time College to teach English. She had looked forward to retirement, thinking it would free her from having to go to work. But when the party secretary told her to report immediately to the Spare-time College, she realized she had to do as she was told.

She must have been hoping for the opportunity to slow down. She pointed out she had never taught before. So she was first sent to audit the classes given by a teacher by the name of Li, in order to learn from him. Then she decided to do as good a job of teaching as she could and paid close attention to Li's methods. At the same time she drew on her own resources, including her studies in psychology. Very soon she won the acclaim of the students only to discover that

Between the close of the 1950s and start of the 1960s, Daisy's eyes express caution and uncertainty. Taken by the former Skirsvky photographer's, by then renamed the Hong Ying photo studio.

Li had developed a hatred for her, particularly when his students skipped his classes to attend hers. She realized this was the envy of one teacher for another, but did not worry about it.

Then the Four Clean-Ups Movement began and because of her husband, Daisy was made a target. A work team arrived from Peking and Daisy was the first target to be selected. The work team had no knowledge of Daisy, so on the basis of the verdict in her husband's case they decided that Daisy had master-minded all his activities. Woo Yu-hsiang was already dead but Daisy had gone free.

In her memoirs, Daisy wrote:

Before long I realized that was exactly what they wanted me to do, confess my sins.

Every afternoon 2 members of our department, one a party member, would take me to a small room for a few hours grilling. I was told to confess all. Then in the evening I had to write down all I had said and hand in the statement the next day.

They would ask me to relate things that I knew nothing about. If I said I did not know they accused me of lying or refusing to confess. This went on day after day. Once I went to the clinic to get some medicine. The doctor sensed that I was under strain. He was sympathetic and gave me some tranquilizers. I took 2 pills instead of 1, and actually found myself falling asleep during the afternoon questioning. No more tranquilizers for me!

In the evenings the teachers held meetings to decide how to run the movement. I was not allowed to participate as they were probably deciding how to deal with me. I was put in a small room by myself. When the meetings were over, I was told to go home.

One evening I seemed to have sat in the small room for hours without being told I could leave. Finally I ventured out only to find the place in pitch darkness except for the room where a cadre on duty sat. I must have startled him when I appeared.

"What are you doing here?" he demanded.

I told him I was waiting for permission to leave when the meeting was over.

"It ended long ago," he said. "You'd better go home."

They had forgotten all about me!

When I got home at night I would get out my typewriter and begin to draft the required article. Sometimes I wanted to rebel and refuse to write, but my son would tell me,

"Mummy, you have to write, go on and finish your writing."

I'd grit my teeth and write and write.

He always helped me, just as he did when I was crushing stones. During the movement to produce steel from scrap iron I was sent off for 3 months. All day I had to break rocks and large stones into small pieces. At times my son would drop by to help me break up some of the large pieces, which I could not handle.

With Daisy as the target, the Four Clean-Ups Movement rapidly got under way in the Spare-time College. All classes were stopped.

Every day the teachers held long meetings. All were required to speak out and criticize Daisy, even if they did not know her. Otherwise they would be labeled as sympathizers. We can no longer judge those people today on the basis of our customary moral standards. Under pressure most of them looked for ways to protect themselves, before they thought of not hurting some one else. But most of those teachers were weak-willed. To continue to make excuses for them today is to besmirch the souls of future generations as well as our own moral standards.

It was not everybody who behaved like this in order to show how untarnished they were. Others seized the opportunity to attack Daisy for the sensation of striking someone who was already down in order to promote their own selfish interests. Li, the teacher who lost his students to Daisy, always spoke. He was always able to transform the tiniest incident into a drama of soul-stirring and life-like events, pushing the criticism meeting to a high-tide.

The best way out for a jealous individual was to press his opponent into a position of no defense and no opportunity to resist. That's how the selfishness behind some impassioned faces at the criticism meetings became revealed as the greatest motive power behind the revolutionary movement of the masses.

Those dark passions were released like the explosion of sewerage pipes, at times comparable to volcanic eruptions.

Now I understand how jealousy sometimes occurs within the same ranks while at others it may be sparked off by totally different social backgrounds. Someone with no possibility of becoming a beautiful young girl from the Kwok family but nevertheless yearns for such a life will indulge in the wildest fancies, become envious and discontented. She will make use of a political movement to express her envy and discontent only because she cannot become like the one she is tyrannizing. In fact, sometimes what appears to be pure and clean has its source in a base personal background.

When I was very small I was taught to control my behavior so as never to offend anyone else. Very often those who taught me suffered in the Cultural Revolution. Thinking back now I realize that their dissimilar faces all shared expressions of modesty and courtesy. In fact each of their faces was like the cover of the box of wonders. It dawned on me that they knew how any careless offense, including even one's own natural advantages, could be turned into a fatal disaster. Their understanding of human affairs included the good and the bad.

But Daisy went through all these trials when the Cultural Revolution was still two years away.

With the onset of the Cultural Revolution she went back to cleaning the women's toilets. Many accounts written by women communist party officials have told how insulted they felt at being compelled to clean the toilets. Daisy understood this. It was not that this work itself was demeaning. What was intolerable was the way others associated you with the smelly and dirty toilets and forced you to clean them. During the Cultural Revolution, Daisy was separated from the ranks of the capitalists for a time and sent to do farm work with women officials who were "put to one side." But she still had to carry away the buckets of excretions, empty them into the cesspools and then wash them. Although the women officials she was working with were not particular, the political difference between Daisy and them had to be distinguished. Daisy was no longer able to carry a full bucket by herself, so every day one of the other women would help her to move the bucket to the edge of the cesspool, after which Daisy had to do the job by herself. Many of these women had served as members of the Four Clean-Ups work team. In those days when they were in power, they were forcing others to do the work of cleaning the toilets.

I do not know if any of those women officials ever wondered how Daisy became such a skilled toilet bucket cleaner.

With the opening up of China after the Cultural Revolution, the story of Daisy's experiences in China over dozens of years circulated abroad. During the 1980s overseas journalists came to Shanghai to find her. By this time Daisy's living conditions had improved. She was living alone in a quiet lane, sharing a kitchen and toilet with her neighbor, while her eyes still twinkled as before.

Hong Kong journalists wrote in their dispatches that Shanghai's Miss Kwok was living in a room measuring a few square meters, and could no longer support herself but had to rely on her relatives and friends abroad. Daisy became infuriated over these reports. She said she did indeed have a house before. Although she was now living in only a small room, it was not just a few square metres. She had lost all her possessions and jewelry, her American dollars and gold bars, but she was most certainly not relying on the support of her relatives in America. After the Cultural Revolution the government returned some of her property which she divided between Jingshu, Zhongzheng and herself, according to the Woo family custom. By this time Zhongzheng was already in the United States so she deposited the value of his share in a foreign currency bank.

"Journalists are the biggest liars," she said.

A television crew from the British Broadcasting Company arrived in Shanghai to interview Daisy. They asked her to take them to the Kwok family home in Lucerne Road so they could make a film there. Daisy did so. When they asked her how much her monthly pension was and how much it would be worth in English pounds, Daisy asked if they knew how much a Chinese needed to live on. They were unclear on this point, so Daisy said:

"I don't want to tell you."

She said later that if she had told a lie she would not have been true to herself. On the other hand, had she told them the truth, the British people would be shocked. They would think it was impossible to live on that amount. They had no idea of the low cost of housing in China. But the BBC journalists insisted that after living so many years in China, this Miss Kwok had lost her nerve.

Next came the host of the top American news program "Sixty Minutes," Mike Wallace. He arrived in China to interview Deng Xiaoping in Peking. Then he went to Shanghai seeking to interview Daisy. The story of Daisy's long years of suffering was already circulating abroad. Wallace wanted Daisy to tell of her life in mainland China under conditions that were unimaginable to people living in capitalist society. Daisy met Wallace but they did not talk for very long because Daisy decided to break off the interview.

She said: "I didn't want to exhibit what I suffered to foreigners. They don't really understand. The more pitiful they can make me the better for them. Because this enables them to feel they are leading a wonderful life."

Daisy became wary of the foreign media after this. Former red guards had already gone to the United States and had had books published, many of them presenting China as a totally inhumane dog-eat-dog society. Daisy said she wanted to retain her self-respect.

Chapter Twenty-eight

1968
Fifty-nine Years Old

A Bowl of Plain Noodles

She tried her best to remain calm and avoid emotional language but she was no longer at ease. She was like a child who had fallen and cut her knee. Despite the pain she obviously dared only take a quick glance but not look directly.

*T**he Cultural Revolution began in 1966.*

This time I felt a difference in the atmosphere. People were rushing here and there when I reached Nanjing Road. Near Henan Road I saw the sign boards of the well-known silk shop Lao Chia Fook being pulled down. They were set on fire right in the middle of the road. The crowds were shouting with glee. This was my first experience of getting rid of the four olds. Soon I was to learn how the capitalists would be dealt with.

I was considered a capitalist though I was only an English secretary in the company.

Daisy's salary of 148 yuan a month was now cut to 24 yuan. Of this amount 12 yuan was intended to cover her own living expenses and the other 12 yuan was for Zhongzheng's. He was then a student at Tongji University. But the university demanded he should pay 15 yuan for this purpose. So Daisy had to deduct 3 yuan from her allowance.

I had to pay half of my monthly bus tickets, another 3 yuan, so I ended up with 6 yuan a month.

Living on 6 yuan a month was no easy task, Barely enough for food. I did not eat breakfast, and had lunch in the school mess hall, picking the cheapest dish. On my way home I would drop in at Pearl's and have dinner there. She wasn't much better off than I, but her husband, son and daughter-in-law together had more than I. The Red Guards found out that I was seeing my sister and accused me of making "underground connections." They forbade me to go there again.

I could not bear a second meal in the mess hall, with the red guards jeering at me all the time. I found a cheap restaurant near the old city wall, which served noodles. The first time I went there I looked at the menu pasted on the wall:

shredded meat with noodles .... 23 fen

salt vegetable with noodles ..... 13 fen

plain noodles .... 8 fen

My mouth watered at the first item. Too expensive. The second item wasn't too bad and cheaper. After reflecting a moment, I realized I couldn't even afford that, so I settled for a bowl of plain noodles for 8 fen.

In 1996, when Daisy told me about the plain noodles, she gently inhaled as though sniffing the scent of a rose and said:

"Oh, it smelt so good, with chopped-up shallots floating in the clear soup in a big steaming hot bowl. I always finished it. I would sit there in the small shop which was always warm in winter. Then I'd go home to my little attic."

By now Daisy had dispensed with her household staff. But in order to give them adequate severance payments, she had had to sell Zhongzheng's camera.

Then in December 1966 she and Zhongzheng were driven out of their home. They were not allowed to take all their winter clothes with them. Zhongzheng had to leave behind the set of toy soldiers his father had obtained from the Enemy Properties Bureau. They were only permitted to take with them a few essential pieces of furniture. Daisy chose a selection of kitchenware, which she thought would be the most useful. They were placed in a container with two drawers, which once held a silver table service that was confiscated when their house was searched. After the knives and forks had been taken away, Zhongzheng had used the two drawers to keep his negatives. However, when the red guards came in 1966 to check over the contents of the kitchenware, they turned over the cover of the container, which covered up the two drawers. The guards did not notice the negatives.

A Shanghai street scene at the beginning of the Cultural Revolution revealing that all is not well. Despite the lights, the street reflects disquiet, with pedestrians walking along the roads instead of the footpaths. Sometimes the lights cut like knives as they tried to escape to narrow and dark places to avoid the lights.

When Zhongzheng returned home he realized at once the significance of what Daisy had done. In 1984 when he went to the United States he took the negatives with him. He brought back copies of the prints when I decided to write this book about Daisy and they became an important part of this volume.

Their new home was a north-facing 3 x 2.4 square meters attic. However, as Zhongzheng was then a student of civil engineering he designed and built a mezzanine floor so that his mother could have a place of her own in which to bathe and avoid using the public toilet. This was the first time for Daisy to share one room with her grown-up son. It was also the first time she had to share washing facilities with others. There were holes in the ceiling and Daisy spent the winter of 1966 here. On clear days the sun shone through the holes. But when the north wind blew Daisy would find her face covered in frost in the mornings.

In January 1967 the red guards destroyed the grave-site of the Kwok family in the Shanghai suburbs. They prized open the brass coffins of George Kwok Bew and his wife. Zhongzheng hurried there as soon as he heard about the destruction but the grave-stone and the large stones surrounding the site had already been knocked down. All the coffins and remains had disappeared, including the chest of Woo Yu-hsiang's ashes. They were never found.

Both Jingshu and Zhongzheng felt Daisy decided in 1985 to do-nate her remains to the Shanghai Red Cross Society for scientific research and not to retain any ashes because she did not want to have her remains dug up one day. Another reason, they thought, was because she would not be able to rest in peace with her parents and had nowhere else to go.

Several months later, in July 1967, Daisy was sent to work as a saleswoman selling water-melons, peaches and eggs in a fruit shop belonging to the foreign trade department, just outside the former French Park in Shanghai's old French Concession.

We sold whatever fruit there was. At that time it was mostly peaches, different varieties. Customers often asked me which were the sweetest, but I couldn't tell. One day, as the shop was closing, I bought one of each kind and tried them. When fruit shops closed for the day fruit was much cheaper, so I was able to buy them. The next day I was able to recommend which were the sweeter peaches, and the custom-ers were pleased with the service I gave them.

When it came to selling the eggs she asked the old shopkeeper for his advice. That was how she learned that by holding the egg under a light she could see whether the yolk was whole or not. There were too many eggs and with no refrigeration they spoilt very easily in the summer. Dissatisfied customers often returned with bad eggs they had cracked open and wanted them replaced. So she learned to differentiate between the good and bad eggs and helped the buyers to select the good ones. The customers began to trust her and returned again and again.

The road directly north of the little egg stall led from Huaihai Road (the old Avenue Joffre) to Nanjing Road, passing a tall old-style building. That year many who could no longer stand the many upheavals went to this building to commit suicide and the building became called the "suicide building." But Daisy's trials and tribulations began much earlier, in 1958. By 1967, ten years later, out of the depths of her misfortune her situation had become even crueler. What was so amazing was that she did not turn to suicide. Instead, she adjusted herself to her fate, avoiding sharp encounters whenever possible, miraculously enabling herself and children to see that life was not entirely without hope. This was the Miss Kwok who in the 1920s was accompanied by a bodyguard and rode in a bullet-proof car. But by 1967 she had learned how to protect herself and her children in times of danger.

That year Pearlie was severely beaten up by the red guards. When Daisy went to see her, she found Pearlie sitting by herself in a dark place, her face and hands covered with bruises. She next discovered that the red guards climbed into Pearlie's house through an open window. They came and went at will and abused her.

Daisy left behind a draft of her memoirs, which on my last visit she gave me written permission to use, along with her photos. She told me that when she recovered she planned to re-write her memoirs. However, she made it clear that she wrote them not for publication but to inform the next generations about her life. However, after she reached the Cultural Revolution in 1966, her account appeared hasty and careless, jumping from one subject to another. Her description of the Four Clean-Ups was still orderly. But when it came to writing about the Cultural Revolution, although she avoided emotional language, she was decidedly no longer at ease. Despite the pain, she dared only take a quick glance but not look directly.

It was in these sections that she suddenly inserted recollections of her childhood. At first this appeared chaotic. Thinking about what she had told me, however, I noted that she actually said very little about the Cultural Revolution. She had once said that recalling the Cultural Revolution was like going through it all over again and this was very painful. Even though 30 years had already passed, and she was in America facing the typewriter and paper, she could not do it. She was like a swimmer swimming the frog stroke with her head submerged in water, having to lift the head out of water after a stretch to take a deep breath. She had to get out, so she would return to her childhood.

Even in her childhood memoirs she did not use emotional language. But her narrative became simpler, and her recollections more distinct, revealing a little girl's heart beating with love for her father and the family's ponies. She could not help turning back to the blue skies of Australia where she spent her childhood. Those early days in Shanghai, including her smooth years at McTyeire and the proud days she spent at Yenching, were not the places she wanted to escape to.

When Daisy was informed in 1968 that Zhongzheng had been declared a reactionary student at Tongji University and placed under house arrest, Daisy had to deliver to this pseudo jail the clothes he needed. Like her early visits to the jail where her husband was incarcerated, Daisy went every month to the university. Formerly it

Members of the Kwok Bew family in the United States in 1968. Percy is leaning over Mary, his still very attractive wife, and Elsie, wearing white earrings and still glowing with the beauty that won her the first Miss Shanghai competition. The photo below shows Daisy and Pearlie in the same year in a different environment. Their hair is already grey, and they are wearing different clothes.

was Zhongzheng who went to the No. 1 Jail on behalf of his mother. But no one could take Daisy's place now. On the way from her home to the university, what did she think? No one knows. What were her feelings? She never said. But she never missed a visit.

Daisy often made use of the night-time. During the day she avoided going back to home or going out from home as much as possible. She tried to avoid the red guards who were stationed at the entrance to the lane where she lived. Seeing her, they gleefully set about tormenting her as a rabbit of prey. But when driven to a point of no retreat, Daisy stood up to them.

Every time Daisy left the entrance to the lane she was required to spend 15 minutes standing before Mao Tse-tung's portrait. She had no watch so did not know how long she had been standing and had to wait till the red guards let her pass. Then she had an idea. She took her alarm clock with her and that day the red guard on duty said:

"Time's up. What are you standing there for?"

Daisy took her clock out and showed it to him, saying:

"You're wrong! There are still 3 minutes to go."

However, in her memoirs about this year of chaos, all she wrote was the following account:

I'm going to relate here a story regarding a person who, like me, realized it was not wise to try and argue or reason with anyone:

A doctor who was a head of a hospital was on his way to work. He went by bus. (Cars were no longer used by capitalists or intellectuals). Every morning his wife gave him a 5-fen coin for his bus fare. She put it in his pocket. Buses are always very crowded, and the doctor had to stand. He tried to put his hand into his pocket to get his 5-fen coin, but instead he put his hand into the pocket of the passenger standing beside him. The man immediately shouted that there was a pick-pocket on the bus. The bus stopped and the doctor was taken to the police station. When questioned he gave his name and that of the hospital where he worked. A Party member of the hospital immediately came to the station to find out what had happened to the head of their hospital. The doctor explained.

"But why didn't you tell the bus conductor?" he was asked.

"Because if I had tried to explain, they would not have believed me, and might even have beaten me up. I thought it safer to admit my guilt."

This is all that Daisy wrote about 1968.

During 1968, Daisy's family in the United States lost touch with her and Pearlie, but they saved photographs for them. One was of a family gathering showing a very sunburned Percy, as though just returned from a holiday by the sea. Big sister-in-law did not appear old. Elsie still retained her captivating beauty and style of the first Miss Shanghai beauty contest. Their children had grown up in America and were not used to speaking in Chinese.

Eventually Pearlie and Daisy died in Shanghai. Of the 8 siblings they were the only ones who remained in Shanghai. Both donated their remains to the Shanghai Red Cross Society, signing their names in Chinese in the donors' book as follows:

"I, of my own free will, donate my remains unconditionally to medical and scientific research for the country's medical education and to improve the treatment and prevention of disease as my last contribution."

But nobody believed that in signing these declarations they were in full accord with the contents.

Some said they had lived the life of parasites, which they wanted to deny. That was why they were able to do what most people could not do. Still others said it was because they had no family grave-site and therefore no place to rest in peace.

Chapter Twenty-nine

1969
Sixty Years Old

Pride and Perseverance

Individuals not suffering for the benefit of the public can still retain their dignity. As an ordinary woman Daisy was doing just this, in order to retain her own unblemished record and avoid causing her children further suffering.

One of Daisy's pho-
tos is from the City of
Shanghai bus ticket she
used. But from 1969
she no longer needed to
deduct 3 yuan from her
monthly living allowance
for this purpose. Instead
she was sent to the East
Wind Farm on Chong-
ming Island to be re-
formed through labor.

She was the first
woman from the foreign
trade department sent to
Chongming Island. As
there was no room for
her to live with the male

Daisy used this photo on her monthly bus pass in the 60s.
Her beauty as well as the torment she suffered may still
be detected, like a blown-out dust storm.

capitalists already there she was lodged with the women cadres who
were in charge at the farm. She learned that her fellow inmates referred to the farm as "the concentration camp." The women cadres did
the same. During the Pacific War the Japanese had intended to send
the 20,000 Jewish refugees who had fled to Shanghai to this little
island and had built a death camp for them there. But in the end this
plan was not carried out.

In her memoirs Daisy wrote the following:

*Cleaning the wooden commode was one of my daily tasks. A cadre was sup-
posed to work with me each day. There were seven of them, so a different one helped*

me carry the commode to the edge of the pit everyday. That is far as they would go. After that I had to empty the commode into the pit, carry it to the stream and wash it and then carry it back to the dorm. The commode was big with no handles, so you can imagine what difficulty I had carrying it alone. Once some youngsters working on the farm criticized the cadres by saying it wasn't right for them to make me work alone, but that was the cadres' idea of how I should be treated in order to remold myself. The youngsters said.

"We think they need remolding themselves."

I could make no comment.

It was also one of my duties to fill the thermos bottles every morning. The cadres expected me to fill theirs as well. One day I slipped and broke one of their bottles. I had to buy 2 thermos vacuums for the bottles as that is what they expected me to do. That was a big part of the 6 yuan I had to live on each month.

After a few months Daisy was transferred to another farm where she also had to work with reformed capitalists. The reason was that the women cadres were leaving to go to a May 7th Cadre School :

As usual I had to follow orders, but I was getting used to the life at this farm and found all the capitalists there were friendly and easy to get along with. I did not cherish the idea of moving.

As I saw it, Daisy's first few months on Chongming Island were filled with terror. She was as good as alone and exposed to a pack of wolves. It was the second time she had left home to be reformed through labor. The first time, however, she was with fellow sufferers. When she was recalled to Shanghai by the Public Security Bureau a young woman risked speaking out and warned her that she should first consider how to protect herself. This fellow feeling was the greatest encouragement she experienced in the face of danger.

While living with the women cadres they would bully her whenever they felt like it. Not for one minute, nor in any corner, could she relax. Those days must have been even more terrible than being in jail. Yet Daisy did not lose her mind, she did not commit suicide, she even insisted she got used to living like that. She still retained her interest in new things. During the winter when all the labor was transferred to dig up mud from the river, she put her name down too, "because I was curios," she said.

I cannot imagine what she relied on. Years later, however, Daisy recalled that compared with the new farm she moved to the original one was much better. At the second farm, their life was more difficult—they had to start work at five, with no breakfast. The cadres supervising them would change every 6 weeks, each guided by their own likes, mood and style. There were no regulations.

The cadres seized every opportunity to criticize whatever the capitalists did, to let them know every day that what they did was wrong. Even when they worked in the fields, if anyone asked how the work should be done, he would immediately be shouted at. Everyone got used to keeping quiet and not to argue back.

This is how Daisy behaved. She kept before her the example of the doctor on the bus.

Under these circumstances, Daisy witnessed the internal strife that went on among the capitalists, how they would sell each other out, how although they were sleeping side by side. They would become enemies for the slightest reason when under pressure. They would not hesitate to harm somebody else in order to make a good impression on the cadres. Once Daisy saw an elderly capitalist bury a hard-boiled egg in his rice to heat it up because he could not swallow it. But someone immediately reported on him, saying that he was a glutton and wanted to enjoy it on the quiet. Now Daisy realized she had arrived somewhere far worse than she had been before.

One day, as the reformed capitalists were laying out rice straw to dry in the fields, Daisy forked open her last stack and discovered a nest of little mice under it. She was always afraid of mice and screamed. Her cries startled the mice that scattered, leaving behind the just-born baby mice.

"Kill them, kill them," her capitalist work-mates shouted, but Daisy could not. So they rushed over and bashed them.

Now Daisy realized she had to take steps to protect herself, to do something that would put her in the good books of the cadres without harming anyone else. Her opportunity came the next time the cadres abused her as a foreign slave for her inability to write about herself and big character posters in adequate Chinese. She responded by declaring that from then on she would make a serious study of Chinese so as to be able to study Mao's works, write posters and material about herself, as well as read the Chinese papers. The cadres were horrified with the first results. Half the characters were written incorrectly. She then took the newspapers to the cadres and asked about the characters she did not know. Eventually they became interested in her efforts but abused her while teaching her. She had never encountered anything like this in high school or university, nor had she achieved anything like this in the close to ten years she had been required to write about herself. It was the first time she had studied so hard. As a result of her efforts she learned from the newspapers to use Chinese both in speaking and writing. Actually nobody knew how much Chinese she really knew and how much she had learned while being abused. When others tried to find out she would look at them sincerely and say with certainty that her Chinese was still not good enough and she did not understand what they meant:

(One day) A meeting was held to decide which capitalist had progressed most. Some named each other. The supervising cadre said,

"Hadn't you forgotten someone?"

SILENCE.

Then he said, "Has no one noticed how Guo Wanying has progressed?"

He told me to go ahead and tell them how hard I had worked to improve my Chinese.

I said, "It was entirely due to this Cadre who had criticized and forced me to learn Chinese. This was the best kind of forcing I had ever had. If he hadn't shown me the way, I would never have improved."

He was very pleased with himself.

One of the people who worked with Daisy at this farm said there was no doubt this "old foreign woman" was a worthy 1934 graduate of the department of psychology at Yenching University. She was able under such dreadful conditions to retain her self-respect, satisfy the cadres' sense of achievement and domination, leaving behind a favorable impression of their reforming methods without harming anybody or wounding herself, as well as persevering to remain alive as well as comforting and encouraging her own children.

I asked myself what I would have done.

Talking to Daisy about this one day, I said probably I would have committed suicide. But she shook her head and said:

No you would not. Without any experience you would think the situation was fearful, but once you went through it, you would lose all fear. Truly! Then you would realize that an individual can become very resolute , or more so than you can imagine.

Probably this was the reason why Mae, just over 20, was so astonished when Daisy passed away at the age of 90. She was virtually brought up by Daisy and believed that Daisy was different to everybody else, that even death could not conquer her.

After enduring such dreadful experiences, dangers, heartbreaks and unimaginable situations that faced the Fourth Miss of the Kwok family, in the end there she was sitting up sedately and smiling before you, delicately sipping a cup of black tea, her soft white curls emanating a certain fragrance. You wondered if there was anything else she could not endure.

She still held her chin up but her old fellow students at McTyeire and Yenching who described her as arrogant don't say that anymore.

Had she been a communist party member in difficulty, I imagine she would have relied on her faith and determination to live on, just like Sister Jiang.

Had she been a persecuted religious believer, like so many nuns in the Middle Ages, she would have turned to spiritual comfort. But Daisy was not any of these, nor was she a far-sighted intellectual with high aspirations. She was more an intellectual housewife. She was only a girl who happened to grow up in the midst of plenty. She was the Fourth Miss of the director of a department store. When the Japanese occupied Shanghai, in order to avoid them she gave up her job and became a young mistress and stayed at home. She was far more suited to favorable conditions, fragrance, praise and delicacy. It was she who Kang Tongbi went out of her way to teach the use of a wire toaster to turn out golden brown toast, requiring only a quiet table and a bright coal fire. But the education Daisy received from facing money problems, and from enduring insults towards her person, and even from witnessing the unfortunate little mice, all belonged to a kind of pride she had that "nothing has frightened me" and "nothing can stop me."

I grew up on the story of Sister Jiang from the time I was small and I was amazed to discover that even without following a faith a person can still become firm and tenacious. Even someone not suffering for public benefit can retain a stubborn dignity. As an ordinary woman, Daisy refused to destroy her own purity, nor would she add to her children's unhappiness in the slightest on her account. I think one of the important reasons why she did not commit suicide was because she did not want to hurt her children.

I do not know what Jingshu and Zhongzheng thought because they never mentioned this, and their mother kept all her feelings to herself. Or did they believe she was a true Pollyanna?

Chapter Thirty

1971
Sixty-two Years Old

Retirement with Honor

It was proved I was not a capitalist. They were the ones who confirmed it! But like all capitalists I suffered a lot, and they were the ones who made me suffer. This certificate is the proof.

The first time I went to Daisy's home I noticed a picture frame hanging on the wall, an old-style frame belonging to the 1970s. It displayed Daisy's certificate of honorable retirement. I always thought only retired industrial workers would go to the trouble of displaying their certificates of retirement on the wall. I never expected to see one in Daisy's home.

But Daisy was very proud of it.

In 1971 she was retired and allowed to return home from the Chongming Farm. This meant her life in a concentration camp was over and she could command her own space. An older person who had spent a few years in a May 7th Cadre School told me how excited they were when informed they could return home for good. Their first impulse was to turn round and rush to the bus stop. I assumed that Daisy would be even more eager than older people with longer battling experience. But instead of jumping with joy to finally leave the people and place that had imposed so much suffering on her, Daisy did not immediately decamp. When the excitement settled down she went to the leadership and requested to be given a certificate of retirement with honor, which all retirees were entitled to.

She was told she was a capitalist

Daisy reasoned that she was born in a capitalist family and was also a member of the family of a capitalist but she herself was not a capitalist. She had only worked in her husband's company as the English secretary. Her name was not listed on the records of the company, nor did she have any shares. She had no power of decision in the company.

The leadership's reply was that all Daisy's claims had to be verified by the original company staff. She then went off to find her former company associates and they provided her with the proof she

213

Daisy by the side of her certificate of honorable retirement. But where does the travel-worn expression come from?

needed.

The result was Daisy became recognized as a retired staff member and from then on ceased to be regarded as a capitalist. In the same year she was awarded this framed document that certified her "retirement with honor." None of the other capitalists who retired and returned home in the same year as Daisy were given the framed certificate. She had a photo of herself taken beneath hers.

The day she received the certificate she declared:

"It was proved I was not a capitalist and by them. But I was treated like all the other capitalists and had to eat all the bitterness. It was they who did it to me. This certificate is the proof."

This is why the certificate was hung on the wall in Daisy's room for years. Her children let it hang there until she passed away.

214

Chapter Thirty-one

1974
Sixty-five Years Old

Grandma Is Special

She was always energetic. Everyone wanted to be with her. It was boring if she wasn't at the gatherings of relatives. Even in restaurants the waiting staff couldn't take their eyes off her.

*I*n 1965, when Daisy was going through the socialist education or Four Clean-Ups Movement, Jingshu, who was in Peking, decided she wanted to marry a footballer. Her boyfriend was from an ordinary family in Shanghai. When Pearlie heard of this she wrote to try and stop the marriage. However, Daisy made it clear that so long as Jingshu loved the boy it was all right and so they got married. It was just like so many years before when Daisy had supported her sister Elsie's choice.

After Zhongzheng graduated in 1970, he was allocated a job as an ordinary worker in Fengyang (Anhui Province) and married the daughter of his master worker. This took place when Daisy was working at the Chongming Farm and studying Chinese for all she was worth during her spare time. Zhongzheng's girlfriend had been introduced to him by his master worker because he sympathized with Zhongzheng's unfortunate situation, as well as liking him. Daisy wrote to Zhongzheng and asked him to consider whether the differences in their educational and social backgrounds might affect their lives in the future. But Zhongzheng, with his 1964 and 1966 experiences behind him, replied saying:

"The educated ones are the worst, the wicked- hearted intellectuals. It is the workers who can be truly kind-hearted."

Daisy said no more after that. When she got leave from the farm she went to Fengyang to visit Zhongzheng and his wife. The day she arrived the people of this little town gathered to see the capitalist lady from Shanghai. They said that she was better looking than Zhongzheng's young wife. So after that Daisy only wore a blue jacket whenever she visited Fengyang. After her retirement in 1971 she would stay in Fengyang for 3 months at a time to help take care of their little daughter, Mae. Daisy also spent 6 months every year in Peking helping

Only these two children could explain why they found their gray-haired grandmother so striking.

Jingshu with her two children, Feng Feng and Ya Ya. When she went to Peking she often took Mae with her so as to lighten the burden of Zhongzheng and Feng Lin. I think this was how she expressed her love and care for those who joined her family out of love during its greatest time of difficulty. In fact, from the time Mae was small and up to primary school she spent much time with Daisy. When Zhongzheng and his family went off to the United States, Mae was temporarily left with Daisy to attend middle school. Thus Mae virtually grew up with her grandmother. Daisy kept on her walls Mae's little paper cuts and thumb-sized Japanese cartoons of beautiful women. Daisy's own children were cared for by nurse-maids while she herself took care of the grandchildren, fed them, comforted them at night, took them out to play, taught them English, did all the things that elderly grandmothers do, for which they bestowed on her their love.

After Mae grew up she began to voice her own opinions. She insisted that her grandmother was special—unlike other grandmothers, she never engaged in idle gossip, nor did she neglect her appearance. Outside in the street nobody noticed other grandmothers but her grandmother was admired and listened to. Her enthusiasm drew others to her. It was boring at the gatherings of relatives if she wasn't there. Even in restaurants the waiting staff could not take their eyes off her.

Chapter Thirty-two

1976
Sixty-seven Years Old

Remarriage

They would make an appointment to meet in a tea-house in a park, or at the home of a friend and Daisy always went with Wang.

*D*aisy now considered marrying Oxford University-educated Wang Mengli, who had also taught at the Spare-time College for people involved in foreign trade.

Wang was an old friend and had often helped Daisy out when she was in difficulty. They got along well together. Jingshu thought it was rather like the past when her parents chatted incessantly. Wang was known for his quietness. But now all those close to him said they had never heard him talk so much. Totally unlike Woo Yu-hsiang, however, Wang seemed almost old-fashioned and inflexible. Children were afraid of him.

After Daisy returned to Shanghai from working in the country-side, Daisy and Wang discussed their proposed marriage with her children. Zhongzheng opposed the marriage, saying he could certainly support his mother and did not want her to rely on someone else. But Jingshu believed marriage would improve Daisy's quality of life.

The night before the marriage, Daisy was in Wang's room making preparations for the following day until very late and had no alternative but to spend the night there. So for the sake of propriety she insisted on sleeping with the door open.

After their marriage, they frequently went on trips to beauty spots and tourist areas.

It was now the latter part of the Cultural Revolution and those capitalists who were elderly or in poor health were no longer the focus of attention. This made it possible for old classmates and friends to socialize together again, meeting in tea-houses in parks or in someone's home. Daisy and Wang always joined these gatherings.

Recalling her second husband, Daisy said Wang was a good man, but he was not like YH and they did not have all that much to say to each other. Wang wasn't so much fun. Even after so many years she

Daisy and David Wang (Wang Mengli) holidaying in Hangzhou.

still used this old expression.

Sadly, however, four years after their marriage Wang contracted cancer and Daisy spent her time visiting him in hospital. Two years later, Wang died and Daisy returned to living by herself.

Chapter Thirty-three

1977
Sixty-eight Years Old

Private English Tutor

Suddenly I felt as though I had been hit by something. It was as if those worn-out colonial buildings along Shanghai's streets were coming alive and re-creating the city's history.

$\mathcal{F}$or ten long years big-character posters had been seen everywhere, filling the streets with a sense of foreboding, no matter whether they called for the striking down of Liu Shao-chi or for the smashing of the Gang of Four. In the misty weather that is typical south of the Yangtze River, they hung like shreds of ragged padded clothing from the walls. The paint from the likenesses of Mao's ruddy face and mole on his chin had gradually overflowed, revealing the original grey, Shanghai's usual color.

But by 1977 the paper supplies that had been reserved for the publication of Mao's works were instead being used to print the test papers for university entrance examination. Universities all over the country, which had stopped functioning for 10 years, now resumed their entrance examinations. The country was swept by a euphoria for studying. Characteristic of Shanghai, its young people immediately began learning English. Realizing the importance of English, many organizations started their own classes. The subject of English stopped being the butt of jokes such as "throw it in the gutter." And its importance has not lessened since. On the walls at lane entrances, on tree trunks in side streets, on telegraph poles, where in the sixties accusations were once posted, there appeared in 1977 advertisements by private teachers for students of English. Nobody knew how to write these advertisements. The name and address of the teacher were written in beautiful handwriting. But no teacher would dare to give his whole name in English, often using only a surname. No textbooks were available. Some teachers typed their own on old-fashioned typewriters, such as, *The Matchstick Girl*. But the stationery shops had no correction fluid. If the teacher made a mistake it was crossed out. Some teachers used pre-Cultural Revolution textbooks like Hsu Kuo-chang's English or the American publication, *English*

900 which had quietly been brought to China by returning travelers. Very soon the trendiest students were using simple sentences like "How do you do?"

Daisy was invited by the Shanghai Silicate Research Institute to teach its specialist personnel. This was the first time a government organization had invited her to be a teacher, the first time she had been shown any respect by anyone not of her own origin and background, the respect due to a good English teacher. It was also the first time that she really took a liking to her students. She later said they were her best students, so intelligent, so hardworking, so respectful, and simply thirsting to acquire knowledge of English and the English-speaking world.

In 1977 Daisy and others of her age group began teaching English outside the schools. Apart from her classes at the institute, Daisy

This simply dressed and modest teacher of English sparked off a frenzy for the study of English and contact with the English-speaking world.

taught private students in her home for a living. At first they wanted to learn English in order to sit for the university entrance exams. Later they came to her because they wanted to study abroad. Daisy did her teaching over the little round table next to the window right up to her last summer. She never stopped. She had dozens of students, including doctors, students, office workers, unemployed youth and the children of neighbors, including the grandchild of a former driver of the Kwok family. One by one, they all went overseas. When Daisy was 89 she planned to get in touch with an elderly teacher, aged over 90, who was still teaching English, a graduate of Yenching University, with a view to learning from his experience.

One of the photos taken of Daisy during this period, though slightly imperfect because the newly imported film and fluid were incompatible, shows her with a genuine smile on her face. I immediately thought of her smile at the time of the Tsingyi Fashion Salon. Although she did not wear glasses then, her hair had not turned white, but her eyes showed no trace of evasion. Forty odd years had to pass before one could see her grief turned into a smile. She had a big black loudspeaker belonging to a heavy Sanyo recording machine. It reminded me of my teacher's house. She also had the glass cup she used in winter to warm her hands, the strange cooking smells, the English accent and sentences, and always "yes" instead of the American "yeah."

The faces of the older teachers of English of that period wore a special expression. It was quiteunlike the pedantry of the Chinese language teachers, the seriousness of the mathematics teachers, of the stress the political teachers put on the first-page of the newspaper, or even the romanticism of the music teachers. Daisy's smile was a good example. It revealed modesty, courtesy and elegance, as well as the beauty of old European culture. But only the old teachers of English shared this expression.

Now they really became respected by many young people. They unfolded a new world to us. They not only taught the sentences and vocabulary in the textbooks. Daisy must have been among them. By December, these teachers were using newly imported Sanyo tape recorders to enable the students to hear their own recordings of Christmas carols and oral conversations about Christmas. In November they talked about turkey. Perhaps they took their best students to Huaihai Road (the old Avenue Joffre) to have a proper meal in a western-style restaurant, teaching them how to eat western food. This was how they taught the students to use English as much as possible in the English-speaking world. This is also how Daisy's best student took a cake and a box of candles with him to the class on her birthday. He helped her light the candles and after he helped her blow the candles out, they ate the cake together. She of course would have told her students how they could make a tasty Russian-style cake. I do not know if the English teachers in Peking taught their students in this way. In 1978 it was in my English class that I learned and saw what American tap dancing was. My teacher was over 70. He had graduated from Yenching University and in fact was a college friend of Daisy's.

The students of that period suddenly became mesmerized by the English language, except for very few with specific purposes. Their teachers fascinated them. They aroused the students in the way, for example, that the colonial buildings in Shanghai's streets re-told its history.

My English teacher found an old Christmas card in his dictionary. It was the first time for me to see a Christmas card. He used it to teach the meaning of "merry" and the meaning of Christmas. He said he did this while teaching us *The Matchstick Girl* because he wanted to enlighten us about the life of children in western society. When

This grateful student came with cake and milkshakes on April 2 to celebrate her birthday.

he spoke about Christmas cards and the stars on Christmas trees, his own eyes began to shine, lighting up all the lines of his modest face.

After finishing a section on English grammar, my teacher found more advanced texts, phrases and proverbs for us. One afternoon he taught us a lesson from *New Concept English*. This was the first imported textbook that students were able to buy from 1980 onwards. I noticed in Daisy's house she used brown paper to cover her books. The books inside had all turned yellow. I don't remember what season it was, but one day our teacher taught us the phrase "every cloud has a silver lining." He explained that this was a beautiful natural phenomenon, which represented the beauty of life for the individual. Even though a person's life might appear like a dark cloud, it still had a silver lining to it, the sun would eventually shine through. That day, our teacher hugged the book close to him as if he was leading a great cause and was not just an English teacher.

Daisy said many people came to her, only wanting to learn to speak English. Some had to go abroad immediately; others had been assigned work which required them to liaison with foreigners. Still others thought they should only learn what they needed to use. She never accepted such students. She put them off by saying she could not teach oral English, that she did not know how to teach oral English, that one had to undergo specific training to learn English, it was not like learning a skill.

One of the older teachers who had studied at St. John's University was asked at the end of class about his own student life. Young people then studying English in Shanghai held the view that students from St. John's University spoke more elegant English than the English people themselves. The older teacher immediately switched to English and said in reply:

"If you were learning English from me at the time I would reply to you in English. We always used topics of discussion. So we can make your question a topic. If this is just a question you are asking me, then I am not going to answer it."

During the Cultural Revolution a widely-used saying was applied to people like teachers of English. It went like this: "Like the onions hanging under the eaves, the roots dry out, the leaves rot but the inside never dies."

We were like small little puritans, and it did not seem right to us that these people should wear people's clothing; they were full of revolutionary talk but lived cautiously like the churches that were still locked up. Yet as soon as it became allowed to speak English, teaching English became a very useful pair of hands. It helped to peel off the rotten leaves.

These older teachers of English played an irreplaceable role in linking up with the young people of Shanghai who were studying English in the late 70s. Nobody knows this outside of those of us who experienced it, including those teachers themselves. It was they who suddenly brought rays of light into our student lives. They replanted the contacts and friendly relationships with the western world in our hearts. Perhaps this is why in the following ten years the number of young people going abroad from Shanghai outnumbered by far those of any other city. During the next 10 years the life-style of old Shanghai became the model for a new generation as well as transformed the most unforgettable city in China's multi-faceted culture.

Chapter Thirty-four

1982
Seventy-three Years Old

English Advisor–Daisy

It was like the feeling of islanders at the time of crossing onto the seldom visited mainland. The promises before them enabled them to forget the old drawbridges they had had to cross to escape.

Gradually Shanghai re-established its former overseas trading contacts. Industrial circles were the first to realize the need to contact machine-tool traders abroad in order to import new equipment and even to export their own machine-tools. Units were set up to directly handle such contacts. But very quickly it was found that existing staffs could not handle English correspondence. Former personnel who had done this type of work 40 years earlier were now politely approached to work as specialists, to correct the English correspondence involved, as well as to assist in negotiations.

Daisy was invited by a consultancy to become an advisor in business correspondence after which standard practice in business correspondence was introduced. Helped by her, the younger staff learned

Daisy was the first English adviser to appear in foreign trade enterprises during the 1980s. Did it occur to Daisy back in the fifties, sixties and seventies that one day she would restore the work of English business correspondence in which she once engaged in the Hsing Hua Scientific Instruments Company?

On Daisy's 80th birthday the company employing her as an English adviser gave a party for her as a token of their gratitude for her contribution to their work. It was the first time she was congratulated by her associates and given a birthday present.

to master the art of business correspondence. Naturally, she was no longer addressed as the Fourth Miss, or Madam or even crudely called by her name, unlike in 1967 when the son of their former maid came to ask for his mother's termination payment. Instead she was given the honorable title of Teacher Guo.

At the time Daisy worked in the Jing'an (Bubbling Well) Hotel. The Australian consulate-general was also located there and she got to know the commercial counselor from Australia. They became friendly and jointly put out a fortnightly newsletter called *English Letters*. Meanwhile, Australia's trade in Shanghai gradually developed smoothly.

Altogether Daisy served as an advisor to the consultancy for 10 years. On her 80th birthday the company gave a birthday party for her. There was an enormous birthday cake and songs were sung wishing her a happy birthday. It was the first time in Daisy's life that a business company celebrated her birthday to show their appreciation of her efforts. She had finally become esteemed.

I was visiting St. Petersburg in 1993 just after the armed clash between the Russian parliament and Yeltsin government. The market there was in a state of disarray and the ruble had depreciated. Old ladies were trying to sell a few tomatoes in the icy-cold weather while the department stores had to wrap up a beautiful fox-fur muff in newspaper. I enjoyed Russia but felt saddened to see such depression.

I struck up a conversation in a coffee shop, with a woman university lecturer who could speak English. We discussed the future of Russia. She had slanted eyes and smiled faintly like the girl described by Turgenev, reflecting the fashionable and simple beauty of St Petersburg women, much like the women of Shanghai. She estimated it would take 20 years or one generation to restore St. Petersburg because Russia had already suffered 73 years of disruption. The new generation could not decide where to begin and would have to start all over again. This was the main reason why foreign investors feared to trade with Russia, they had no way to coordinate with each other.

"But your conditions are so much better," she said. "You only had 40 years of destruction. Your old people are still living. You can quickly find ways out."

I had heard it said foreign traders trusted Shanghai business people and regarded them as understanding the rules of trade. But I had never known the reason before. It was in that coffee shop, where the coffee was as weak as water and as sweet at saccharine, that I realized the significance of those old teachers of English and English advisors in today's Shanghai.

I had lost touch with my own teacher of English years ago. So I

Daisy working as interpreter at a trade fair held in the Shanghai Industrial Exhibition Hall.

had no way to let him know this. In fact, I also forgot to tell Daisy about this. My teacher's generation of English teachers was literally "thrown into the gutter." Only now were they allowed to practice their skills. They probably felt they had rediscovered what they had lost and thought no more about it.

Daisy worked up to 1993 in the consultancy when she became 85. That was the year that Shanghai's economy began to accelerate, turning it into the world's greatest exploding city. Many leading world corporations have since set up offices in Shanghai. The young Chinese white-collar workers there were already using overhead projectors and impeccable English in their presentations. Shanghai had become a leading international market place while the fore-runners of this drive were planning to add MBA degrees to their qualifications. "Globalization" was their watchword.

Once on the right track they surged forward. It was like the feeling of islanders at the time of crossing on to the seldom visited mainland. The promises before them enabled them to forget the old sun-bleached and rusty suspended drawbridges they had had to cross to escape. But they still felt some uncertainty as they squeaked their way forward and wondered whether it would all be of any use and lead to broader prospects.

Chapter Thirty-five

1983
Seventy-four Years Old

"It Shows I am Working"

I like this photo. When I die, I would like people to retain this image. This photo shows I am still working.

$\mathcal{D}$aisy spent the last afternoon of her life on September 24th 1998. I was with her deciding which photos could be included in Shanghai Princess. The photos were not easy to come by and reveal much of her ninety years. The first was taken on her one-year old birthday, the last on her 90th birthday at a party hosted by relatives and friends. She is shown standing beside the birthday cake. Almost all the photos were saved by Zhongzheng.

As we sat round the little table before the window and looked over the photos, Daisy said:

"I used to have more than 30 photo albums. During the Cultural Revolution the teachers at the Spare-time College tore them all up. I never wanted photos any more after that, but look, see how many there are now."

She picked up a hastily printed black-and-white one and said:

"I like this photo. It was taken at the Spare-time College They asked me to go back again once a week to make recordings for the oral classes. We didn't have many tapes for recording purposes then. I used to read the texts aloud and then make a recording for learning purposes."

The Spare-time College was where Daisy was ill-treated during the socialist education movement. All her photos were destroyed there during the Cultural Revolution. This school for the staff had a farm and it was the first place where Daisy was sent to "be reformed through labor." The old gatekeeper at the Foreign Trade Department Farm where the school was now re-housed was still there. He used to see her arrive to do manual work and now he saw her coming again to make recordings. They greeted each other cordially and he said:

"I remember you. Aren't you the Fourth Miss of the Kwok family sent to be reformed by labor?"

"I would like to use this photo as my memorial photo because it proves I am working."
—Guo Wanying

Daisy replied:

"That's right. That's me."

Zhongzheng did not want his mother to go back to help out the Spare-time College where she had been so badly treated.

But Daisy still went. Some said she wanted those who had criticized her as worthless to know that she was now considered to be valuable. Others said this just revealed her magnanimity and proved she was useful. But Daisy said nothing.

She obtained this photo in the very place where she had lost all the others.

Caressing the photo, she said:

"I like this photo. When I die I would like people to retain this image of me."

"Why?" I asked.

"This photo shows I am still working."

She focused the magnifying glass on the photo and said:

"See. This is the recording room. There's the microphone. Then I have something in my hands.

It was an old-fashioned microphone and it showed a 1983 copy of an exercise book that was available in all stationery shops. The illustrations were very simple but this did not deter Daisy's pride in herself and in her work.

At last she had achieved independence and gained recognition.

The following day she died in her home. Seven days later Jingshu, Zhongzheng and Mae arrived separately to hold a memorial service for her. This photo was enlarged and placed on view besides Daisy's remains.

Chapter Thirty-six

1986
Seventy-seven Years Old

George Returns

In the search for her piano, Daisy was directed to the suburbs, but the one she found there was not hers. Nor was the one in the nearby city of Suzhou. Then she was asked to go to Guang-zhou, but by that time she was reluctant to make such a long journey.

*I*n 1986 Daisy's youngest brother, George, returned. He was the one who left Shanghai in panic, leaving behind a revolver with the Woo family. In appearance he now looked more like an American of Jewish background. At the same time he expressed a wistful but reticent longing for home. His wife was the beautician who had dressed Daisy's hair for her wedding. The two were now operating a beauty shop in Hawaii.

Daisy took George to see the old house where they had spent their childhood. They went to the old Kwok family department store's annex or Seventh Heaven building, where George used to have his office. They also took a look at the Department Store, now called the Hualian Commercial Building. As of old, it was still regarded as a leading commercial house in Nanjing Road. Daisy used to shop here for shoes. Once when she could not find what she wanted, George, who was then one of the managers, took out his own money and said:

"Go over to Sincere's and have a look. Don't embarrass us here any more. Take the shoes as a gift from me."

She told George that a few years earlier she had been informed that all the items confiscated when her home was searched were to be returned. Included was what she had taken after 1962 from Kwok residences in the Seventh Heaven building for use in the Woo family home. Following the Cultural Revolution the government also began returning items taken away during the searches of people's homes. She had submitted a list of items taken from her, and from then on was frequently asked to go and retrieve them. She learned then that the churches, which had been closed and had been used as warehouses. Daisy's colleagues arranged for a small truck to move the mass of belongings they expected her to recover, but all she was offered was a

George returns to Shanghai. He is sitting between Daisy and Zhongzheng's daughter, Mae, who knows nothing about the past. There is no mention of a revolver or cartridges.

broken white jade ring, which she had never seen before. On another occasion when she was notified to reclaim her jewelry, she was given a bag of jewelry. But when she opened it up she found that most of it was not hers and returned it.

Still another time, all the confiscated items were lumped together. However, she did succeed in finding the safe in which she had kept her stamp collection, but the lock had been broken and it contained a mahjongg set.

Sometimes she was asked to go to distant places in the suburbs. She went to Dachang County to identify her paintings and scrolls of calligraphy. But she took fright when she saw almost a thousand items awaiting identification. About 100 scrolls had been taken from Daisy but when she started looking she quickly developed a headache.

Sometimes she found somebody else's name pinned on one of her paintings. On other outstanding paintings several claimants were listed. The final decision was not to be made till later.

She went searching for her piano in the suburbs, but the one she found was not hers. Then she was told to go to the nearby city of Suzhou, but the one there was not hers either. Finally she was notified to go to Guangzhou. However, by then she was reluctant to make such a long journey.

Woo Yu-hsiang's case was re-examined and he was rehabilitated. The government returned the money that had been deducted from Daisy's earnings on his account. Because of this, for 10 years Daisy had had to survive on only 6 yuan a month.

With a sense of feeling lucky for himself, George asked Daisy about her experiences in Shanghai over the years. Like all other members of the Kwok family who had moved overseas, he believed that had he remained in Shanghai he would have encountered the same unimaginable treatment as Daisy. As far as he could make out, however, compared with Daisy's misfortunes, the panic he suffered at the time of his flight seems like pleasant recollections. Daisy told him a little, then as before she shrugged her shoulders and spread out her arms saying:

"Look, I survived and I survived very well."

He did not ask about the outcome of the three revolvers and Daisy said nothing about them.

Later on I asked Daisy why she had not told George that he had upset everything. But Daisy said:

"He had no intention to hurt us. What would be the use of telling him? In any case they wanted to catch YH out. When they first arrested him nobody knew we had buried the revolver. Even if there were no revolver, YH would have been arrested on some other charge."

Chapter Thirty-seven

September 1989
Eighty Years Old

"Where Shall I Begin Today?"

Much of what happened to Daisy during the long drawn-out Four Clean-Ups Movements and the Cultural Revolution was revealed to her children only through her memoirs.

---

*E*ncouraged by friends and relatives while she was visiting Zhongzheng in the western United States, Daisy started writing her memoirs on his typewriter. She said she was doing it for the children of her
own family. This is how she began:

> *Elsie had written me about Leon's writing an account of our Kwok family*
> *background. She mentioned that she intended correcting some of the statements. It*
> *wasn't until both Elsie and Leon had passed away that I finally got a copy of Leon's*
> *article from George.*
>
> *As soon as I read it I felt that I also wanted to record some reminiscences of*

Daisy with Zhongzheng in the United States in 1989, where she began writing her memoirs. Already a doctor of computer studies, as a little boy he instinctively played the piano in 1958 to reassure his mother he had returned home when he learned the dreaded news that two policemen were talking with his mother upstairs. In fact they were notifying her of her husband's arrest.

my early life. My biggest regret is that Leon's article did not reach me until after Pearlie had passed away, as I would have liked to have consulted with her on many points. I also regret that Pearlie did not read Leon's article as I know she would have enjoyed it very much. Time is passing rapidly and I wonder if I'll be able to put down all I want to record.

Now where shall I begin today?

In order to do a good job of writing up her experiences, Daisy joined a university writing course. Each student was required to produce a piece of writing every week by way of practice. Daisy wrote about how she had learned to make butter in Australia, about the Tsingyi Fashion Salon, the encounter with highway robbers at Hangzhou, the game of "follow the leader" she had learned from Wally, the first breakfast after her marriage, but she never wrote a single word about the Cultural Revolution that had shocked the western world to its core.

"Foreigners do not understand these matters," she explained.

However, she did record her experiences during the Four Clean-Ups and the Cultural Revolution. Many of these incidents her own children first learned about from her memoirs. A foreign friend in Shanghai wanted to help Daisy have her memoirs published, but she would not agree, Jingshu said.

Chapter Thirty-eight

April 1990
Eighty-one Years Old

Childhood Incantation

She returned alone, smiling in the sunshine that once shone on her. But never again would she wear the lacy white dress nor would her shoes be so clean that the soles could not be told from the vamp. Her face was lit up with a deep smile, typical of the elderly.

*M*iraculously, Daisy celebrated her 81st birthday in Australia, and the event was recorded by photographs. That is how we learned that those tall Australian trees do not shed many leaves in the sun and wind, while during autumn in the southern hemisphere the trees are covered with little yellow flowers. Neither do all the chrysanthemum buds fall off. Daisy saw many chrysanthemums in the florist shops, including the simple and white marguerite daisy which she called her flower. It was another of those innumerable autumns when Daisy finally realized the dream of her most difficult days, to go back and see Australia.

During the 1980s Daisy visited her relatives in the United States and Woo Yu-hsiang's family in Singapore, but nothing could

At long last Daisy arrived back in Australia in 1990 where she celebrated her 81st birthday with relatives in Brisbane. Childhood memories flooded back to her, such as making butter in school, like the incantation of a witch's curse.

compare with her return to Australia. She hoped to see the old house she had left in Sydney eighty years ago, No. 2 Croydon Street, when gaslight was still being used. Did she find it? She did not say. If it was no longer there she would not have been surprised. She was no longer the innocent little girl who told her friends:

"Dad is taking the whole family to a Chinese restaurant called Shanghai."

She had long since learned what this distant-sounding word of Shanghai had in store for her. Now she realized it was this clean and bright place here that had been her paradise all along.

The Kwok family used to have two ponies. Elder brother, Leon, looked after the horses for which he was paid two pennies. Later Wally was put in charge but he was not as meticulous as Leon. It was always little Daisy who fed the ponies their grass. In order to win Daisy's submission, Wally said he would give her one penny. Daisy worked enthusiastically and then went to ask for her penny. She put out her hand as Wally had asked her to do. But after placing the penny in her hand, Wally immediately removed it. He said:

"I said I would give you a penny, but I didn't say you could keep it."

Daisy had gone on to experience love and disillusionment. She had tasted what it was like to be the wife of a reckless young man. She had experienced the joys of motherhood with two beautiful children, as well as the trauma of facing a difficult childbirth on her own. Other memories were of the strange jail gatehouse, the time when she went to identify her husband's already unrecognizable body, the cruel battering to death of a nest of mice in the weak sunlight south of the Yangtze river by capitalists undergoing reform through labor, not to mention enduring the turbulence of the times as a daughter from a rich family. She could no longer be angry with Wally. After all, they had shared the happiness and simplicity of their early lives. Of all eight siblings, Wally had been the best brother of all.

Daisy returned to Australia alone, smiling in the sunshine that had once shone on her. But never again would she wear the lacy white dress, nor would her shoes be so clean, because she could not then walk. Her face was no longer unruffled and with the child-like dignity of eighty years ago, her age-revealing skin was covered by the floating smile on her face. She would have told the smiling relatives she was visiting about her childhood and how she had learned to make butter.

Returning to America after visiting Australia, Daisy continued her writing course. This is the story she wrote then:

One morning the teacher showed us a bottle of milk.

"We are going to make butter," she said.

So we all watched her enthusiastically. She gave the bottle to the first child and said,

"Shake it hard for one minute and then pass it on to whoever's next to you."

Each child took it in turn to shake the bottle hard for one minute and then passed it on. Very soon we noticed little bits of butter collecting on the side of the bottle.

"Go on shaking," the teacher said.

Now the bell rang for recess.

"Those who want to go out and play may do so, those who want to continue shaking the bottle may also do so," the teacher said.

Two of my friends came over and whispered to me:

"Let's go and play hop-scotch like yesterday."

I was the only Chinese in the class. It wasn't easy for me to make friends. I was so happy that they liked me, so I agreed and we went and played hop-scotch. When the bell rang again, we went back to the classroom. We found our chairs had been put on one side. The other children were still shaking the bottle. The teacher told us to sit on our chairs. The other children were watching the butter forming inside the bottle becoming bigger and bigger. When the teacher announced that the butter was ready, they all smiled.

The teacher then gave each child a small slice of bread on which they spread the butter they had just made. But we three got nothing.

"This is to punish you for not staying here to make the butter and going out to play," the teacher explained

But it was no explanation at all. It was the teacher who said we could choose, but because we chose what we wanted to do, we were punished.

If Daisy had found the classroom at the Crystal Street school, outside which she had had to stand when she was excluded from the other children, would she have thought any more about it?

Perhaps she did not have time to look for it. Her purpose in visiting Australia was not just to have a look around for old times' sake. Zhongzheng was finishing his PhD studies that year and she wanted him to find a job in Australia. But she failed to do so. However, she obtained an Australian passport for herself, although she did not tell others about it. A year later she was living in Shanghai as a national of another country while Zhongzheng stayed in the United States.

Daisy did not want Zhongzheng to return to China, but she herself returned. This was the most puzzling question to all those who knew what she had been through. Why did she want to return to China? The first time she returned from America she was asked by a middle school to give a talk to their students of English. Some of the students posed this very question to her. Her reply was:

"Because I am Chinese. This is my home."

When Daisy returned after visiting Australia, others asked her since she had been to the place of her birth why did she still want to return to China? She said:

"My whole life has been based in Shanghai. I cannot leave this place. Everything is familiar to me—my doctors, my hairdresser, even my bed."

But the last time Daisy returned from the United States, the doctors warned her of the possibility of a sudden stroke. So she decided not to go to the United States any more, or to Australia. When I asked her about this, she said:

"I haven't got the money to live in Australia. And I don't have the time to rebuild my life again."

With this short explanation she gave me a long, penetrating look.

Chapter Thirty-nine

1996
Eighty-eight Years Old

Daisy and Songlin

You had to judge each person individually, said Songlin, not by class origin. The maid was always telling tales on him whenever he broke the crockery. She hoped he would be punished. But she turned out to be the one who stole the family's U.S. dollars.

$\mathcal{B}$efore their misfortunes the Woo family had a small house staff. Songlin was the houseboy and he came from a coastal village in Southern Jiangsu Province. His job was to run messages, take Jingshu to and from her ballet classes and to play with Zhongzheng. After the People's Republic was set up he went off to work in a factory, but from time to time he would visit the Woo family.

Later on Songlin returned to his home village and lost contact with the Woos. However, after 1976 he returned to Shanghai to work in the same factory as before. Again he went to call on the Woo family, but Daisy was no longer living at that address. It took several Sundays before he learned where Daisy was living. He asked at the office of the lane committee to have a look at the names of the residents, simply claiming to be a distant relative from the countryside.

When he finally found the entrance to Daisy's home both of them shrieked with delight on seeing each other. From then on Songlin often visited Daisy on his day off, to help her tidy up her place and as the seasons changed, to get out the straw mats, or put away the quilts, install the electric fan and other such heavy work. Eventually he also retired and there was no danger of him breaking Daisy's fine porcelain. As Daisy became older she became more dependent on him. If, for example, she wanted to go to the bank, she would wait for Songlin to arrive and go with her. Songlin would go out first and call a taxi. He would place himself between Daisy and any suspicious character who might be lurking around.

"Just like a bodyguard," he said later.

Songlin used to call Daisy Young Mistress but now he did not. At first Daisy did not notice this, then she thought it rather strange, but he could not think of a suitable form of address he might use. He did not dare to call her Teacher Guo like others because he felt he had never been a student and had no right to do so. So he avoided giving her a title by simply going and asking her what he should do. He also refused to accept any payment from Daisy.

"I just went to help her," he said. "She was old, her children were not there and we always got along very well."

As the political situation continued to loosen up, Daisy's old cook also came to look her up. He had stayed with the Woo family right up to the Cultural Revolution when they were driven from their home. Back in 1958, when Zhongzheng returned home one day, it was this cook who told him his mother was being interviewed by policemen upstairs. Zhongzheng wanted to let his mother know he had returned by playing the piano. The cook had rushed out from the kitchen to try and pull Zhongzheng off the piano stool in case he made matters worse. The cook was very skilled at making Fuzhou dishes, which Daisy liked very much. From then on he came to Daisy every week and cooked the whole day for her. He did this right up to the day when he was knocked down by a bicycle, and his legs were paralyzed. He was single and lived by himself. Taking her own baked cakes with her, Daisy found the chef's address and went to see him. She reminded him that when he worked for the Woo family they had told him they would take care of him in his old age, just as the Kwok family did in the case of all their long-serving household staff. Daisy assured him she would take care of him for the rest of his life. She would pay his medical bills and find a nurse to take care of him. She gave him a bank book of money that was to be his. Sadly however, soon afterwards, he committed suicide on his bed. Right up to her death, Daisy always referred to the cook as though he was a member of her family.

Another beneficiary of Daisy's concern was the grandson of an old driver in the Kwok family who was planning to go to England to study. He now came to Daisy to learn English. During the Chinese

Daisy and Songlin attending a new year dinner in 1996 given by a former member of the house staff of the Kwok Bew family. No longer was their relationship that of Young Miss and houseboy, but instead one of firm friends.

New Year Daisy was invited to his family's reunion dinner. She was placed at the head of the table with the family elders and photographs were taken. Among the dishes served were plates and plates of white-cut chicken, deep-fried yellow croaker with sweet and sour sauce.

Whenever Daisy's foreign friends invited her for dinner, they often invited Songlin too.

Songlin took care of Daisy right up to her last day. He slept in what was actually a tiny box-room. Because Songlin was there, Jing-shu, who had been caring for her mother, was able to return to Peking. It was on one of these days that Daisy suddenly felt the urge to have a bowl of the wonton that was being hawked on the street by a vendor. But Songlin refused to buy her a serving. He wanted to make the little meat dumplings for her with meat that he had washed and minced. He was very obstinate about it and Daisy said:

"Songlin, I am no longer the Young Mistress of the olden days."

Songlin paid no attention. He went and made the mince, bought the spinach and made his wonton. But by the time they were ready she had lost her appetite.

"She must have been feeling bad when she died," Songlin said.

"When I washed her face I had to wipe the tears away."

He also sent a wreath to the memorial service but now he had to give her a title. He called her "Old Elder Aunt."

After the service, members of the Kwok family still living in Shanghai had a meal together. Songlin presided and took care of all the guests, including the black-clad Jingshu and Zhongzheng. Jingshu said it was like the olden days when Songlin minded her and her brother. Everyone present drank a toast to Songlin. The women helped him to the choicest morsels on the table and thanked him for taking care of Daisy. They praised him for his tireless work, saying without him they would not have known what to do.

I asked Songlin if he thought he and Daisy came from two different classes. He said:

"You have to judge each person individually, not by class origin. The maid was always telling tales on me when I broke the porcelain, hoping I would be punished. Then it turned out she was the one who stole the family's U.S. dollars and she was from the proletariat. But the young mistress and I got along very well."

Before Zhongzheng left for America, taking with him Daisy's memorial photo and other family heirlooms, he said to Songlin:

"I will take care of you in your old age."

Chapter Forty

1998
Ninety Years Old

God Is Watching over Her

When I mentioned the analogy of the crushed walnut and the esthetic life that must have been so painful for a gentle woman, she looked at me straight in the eyes and said:
  "I would accept whatever life bestowed on me."

*H*olding a bunch of roses, I arrived in Daisy's home on the afternoon of September 24th. I wanted to return to her the last 26 photos, to welcome her back from the hospital and, most importantly, to ask for a few more details before writing up her story. Hunan Road is rather long and green trees covered the lanes along it. At 2 o'clock in the afternoon it was quiet and still. I spotted a small thin sparrow hopping along the street. The hot sweltering summer was already over. I looked through the mass of green leaves at Daisy's wide open window on the third floor. She had not turned on the air conditioner which Jingshu had installed for her, and which Daisy almost never used, as the wide-open window would deliver even more oxygen to her ninety-year old lungs. At the time I thought her heart and lungs were much better. She was waiting for me. Her hair was newly-permed and curled around her face. She was wearing make-up, her way of greeting guests. This was my second visit after she became unwell that summer.

The first time I went to the hospital. But it turned out she did not like others to see her lying in bed, so I waited until she returned. The ward she was in was old and messy. Its green walls seemed to be covered with blemishes. In Shanghai some old people who cannot stand the sweltering summer heat prefer to stay in hospitals. There was a bed in the corridor for an elderly woman outside the ward. She appeared sickly and I dared not look at her. But I noticed she herself did not like having others look at her either.

When Daisy saw me, the first thing she did was to touch her face and say:

"I look awful!"

Actually there was nothing awful-looking about her at all. She just seemed weaker and on the narrow hospital bed she was curled

Zhongzheng and Jingshu with Daisy in hospital on 29 August 1998. There was no change in her appearance in her last days. She still sat upright, was composed and smiling.

up like a ball.

It was a public ward and Daisy longed to return home to her privacy.

Now on my second visit, I found the house very cool. Daisy was sitting in her usual place near her large plum-colored bed. Even when I visited her in the coldest winter, that's where she would sit. She told me how at such times she carried around a heater but when she took off her clothes to go to bed one night, she found the quartz in the heater had burned all her woolen clothes.

This being extremely dangerous for old people, I urged her to get an air conditioner. But she said that hot air always rises and would collect on the ceiling and not be of any use. Besides, it would be a waste of electricity.

I said: "Stop trying to save electricity. If your children knew how you were passing the winter in Shanghai, they would be very upset.

But I don't think she quite got what I meant. She said seriously:

"No, I don't want my children to look after me. Some say my son is in America and would surely want to take care of me. That's not the point. Between my children and myself there is no question of wanting this or that. There is no need for them to take care of me. I have never thought like that. Should they want to do so, it would be because of their affection for me. It is not their duty. I have never wanted my children's money."

I knew this was true. That's why seeing her wearing thin clothes and sitting comfortably in a chair, I felt happy for her. I said:

"You look well."

She smiled and said: "The only trouble is I have no appetite."

I thought this was natural after being seriously ill, so I said the next time, when she would have recovered further, I would take her to La Maison Rouge to have oxtail soup, said to be very nourishing. She said we could also go to a gay bar, which she knew I had intended to go to in the summer and wanted to have a look at. I was so surprised that I laughed out loud and said:

"If you walk into the bar the people there will think it freakish."

She laughed too. Her retort was:

"Why can't I go? I've even been to Hard Rock. I'm just interested in going where I haven't been before."

Yes, true enough, I knew. I also knew she never liked anyone to assist her when she walked, not even when getting on or off public transport. She did not want anyone to help her. Allowing her to take care of herself pleased her. Everyone knew this. Whenever a new acquaintance joined the group taking her out to dinner and there were steps, someone would say:

"Don't try to support the old lady. Let her go by herself."

But I found out from Jingshu, when she wept at the memorial service, that Daisy had climbed up to the third storey all by herself when she returned from the hospital. She would not let even Jingshu help her. She died a few days later of physical exhaustion.

During this second visit I mainly wanted Daisy to tell me more about the 26 photos covering the 60s to the 90s. These photos were taken during her most difficult days. They revealed how she held her chin up, while in her eyes which looked straight at you could be detected her kindheartedness and brave spirit.

Sitting at her old place near the window, Daisy spoke as much as usual. She said she intended to continue writing her memoirs and her story. I told her I wanted her to go over the galley proofs when they were ready. We also discussed how we should keep in touch when she went to Peking for the winter. She said she liked Shanghai because this was where her life was. As we went over the photos, she picked out one showing her making tape recordings for her students. She said she liked this photo and when she died she would like it to be her memorial photo, because it showed her working.

Yes, right up to this summer she was still working and had dispatched a student to England, a grandson of a former driver in the Kwok family.

She told me on this day, September 24th, that she was going to let her students know she had returned home. Thus it could be said she worked until she died. She was an elder who prided herself on her work. Three days later, the photo she chose was enlarged and became her memorial photo.

All along I had wanted to ask if she felt any resentment over all the frustration she had suffered. I first met her in 1996 and began interviewing her shortly afterwards. But I had never heard her

complain. Nor had Jingshu or Zhongzheng. Among those around her, no one really knew how she assessed her life. One day we were almost close to this issue. I brought up the analogy of the crushed walnut and the fragrance that followed its painful smashing. When I mentioned appreciation of the beauty of life and the suffering endured by a gentle woman, she looked at me and said:

"Well, I would accept whatever life bestowed on me."

She never gave a "yes" or "no" answer to this question.

By September 24th, I still wanted to pursue this question. However, the time passed very quickly and after two hours I thought I ought to call a halt, but I still hadn't asked this last question.

So I said: "Next time I'll only ask one question: do you have any complaints about your life?"

She stood up in front of the table and said:

"After I returned from America, various schools invited me to give talks in English. At the Nanyang Middle School one of the girl students asked me why I had returned to China. My reply was: 'I am Chinese'."

I couldn't see Daisy's eyes clearly in the dusk with the reflection from the sunset on her white hair, so I couldn't tell whether she had answered my question or not. Later on I asked Jingshu and Zhongzheng what they thought. They pondered for a while and then said if that was what Daisy said, then she was answering the question.

After talking with Jingshu and Zhongzheng, instead of going home, I went with my husband to call on a fellow student from my university days who had returned from America. While in New York he had made a study of inscriptions on ancient Chinese bronzes and stone tablets in the New York City Museum. He was a calligraphist and we

My last gift of flowers to Daisy was white lilies which I placed beside her memorial photo. White carnations already lay at her feet as a final bidding of good-bye. It finally came to me suddenly as I was dotting the last period to this book how much I owed to Daisy for allowing me to see a soul as fragrant as a flower.

wanted a funeral couplet for Daisy's memorial service. The three of us sat for a long time around Chinese ink. We finally decided on:

有忍有仁，大家闺秀犹在，
(Patience and benevolence live on in spirit,)
花开花落，金枝玉叶不败。
(Flowers bloom and fall, but golden twigs and jade leaves never die.)

It was in that instance that I decided on the title of the book about Daisy.

September 24th was our last day. Daisy saw me off at the landing and everything was the same as before. When she gently waved to me I thought of our first meeting and how we went out to dinner afterwards. She walked between us making us young women feel like clumsy boys. She retained this elegance till her very last day.

Another full day passed and the time for her departure arrived. All this time, she had never uttered a single word of recrimination about her life. Perhaps this was the spirit she wanted to retain.

At dusk on her last day she went to the toilet by herself, then returned to her bed and lay down. A few minutes later she began breathing heavily and then quickly departed.

Daisy remained independent all her life. Her ideal was not to have anyone take care of her. She succeeded in passing away peacefully, neatly and with dignity. In this typical early autumn dusk God had seen her, heard her and finally helped her to realize her wish.

After Daisy lay down on her little bed, she whispered:

"Why am I so tired?"

Postscript

When I finally finished this book and dotted the last period, it was already deep into the night, but earlier than I expected.

Originally I thought it would take me until dawn. Now at last with the conclusion of Daisy's story in the reddening Shanghai night light, I thought of the debt I owed to so many. Without their help and some obscure luck, I could never have written it. This book is truly unlike any other I have written.

First of all, there was Daisy and the two years I spent getting to know her, just chatting with her. While waiting for my daughter to finish her piano lesson, I would go to Daisy's place. Her white hair was like a cloud floating before the window. She was a truly lovable lady; how I pine for her!

Her children are Jingshu and Zhongzheng. Jingshu painstakingly checked the manuscript. Most of the photos were brought back to Shanghai by Zhongzheng from the United States. Jingshu made sure that the manuscript was as accurate as possible while Zhongzheng provided its heart with the photos. Then there were their own recollections, tears and pride.

While I was preparing to write this book I received help from many sources. There were so many of them. Mo Shujun, who helped prepare and restore the photos was the first to hear the full story and to see all the photos. As he squatted before the reprints and studied the old photos, he began to think aloud:

"This old lady is really a jade leaf on a golden twig," he said.

That's where I got the phrase from and it has an important place in the title. He was the one who restored the old photos on a printing press computer. The earliest were more than 80 years old. He would deliver the photos and negatives to my house in the evening with the care of an express service. Carefully removing a large envelope from a still larger bag that hung across his chest, he would say:

"Mission accomplished. Your life is still safe."

I had impressed upon him that if anything happened to the photos my life would be at stake. Every time I thanked him he would say:

"It's just something I did for the old lady."

Everyone who had any connection with Daisy's story and photos put out their hands to help me, the technicians in the photographers', the young girls who worked in color photo processing, most of the staff of reading rooms and local document libraries, as well as researchers on Shanghai's history who knew I was writing the book. Even the taxi drivers.

The day of the memorial service I was carrying flowers and rushing to catch a taxi. A middle-aged driver with a smoke-stained face literally flew me and the flowers to the medical institute road. He said afterwards he had never driven so fast before. It was the story of Daisy that moved those who heard about her by chance.

I consider myself very privileged to have been able to write Daisy's story.

The Sunday in March after I completed the manuscript was a very dull day. I decided to go back to the lane where Daisy had lived.

During her final years, Daisy lived in one room just off a larger lane in a compound of western-style houses. These were divided by slender bamboo fences that emitted a burned fragrance in the sunshine. The soil along the roadsides nourished peach saplings bearing white blossoms and filling the air with fragrance, a sight rarely seen in the city.

It was the first time since autumn that I had returned. When I saw the peach blossoms were already out on the many green trees lining the road, I realized winter had come and gone while I was writing. I slowly followed the trees and flowers till I came to the iron-gate entrance to Daisy's old place. Even if I went up I would not be able to see her. But through my writing this winter I had spent every day with her story and life.

I learned from her the value of kindness and determination. If I only learned a little, I hope that what I learned will be of some use through the small ups and downs in my own life. From the lane to Daisy's house I took in the green-colored window on the third storey, the green iron gate, the quiet trees, the slender black bamboo fence, the thin little white peach blossoms, and I felt comforted. It was as though I knew Daisy was now happy and well somewhere, seemingly wherever Daisy was there were also tiny thin peach blossoms.

My thanks go to Daisy for enabling me to learn how to go through life in the face of wind and waves, to persist in one's integrity and life-style, to maintain an independent spirit throughout life, in good times and bad, and to remain warm-hearted and care-free.

I first met Daisy in 1996. In 1998 I made up my mind to write a book about her. At her memorial service I said I hoped that through my book she would achieve everlasting life. I earnestly hope that I have accomplished this.

20 March 1999
Shanghai

My Mother Daisy Kwok

$\mathcal{T}$en years after the publication of *Shanghai Princess*, an English edition is finally due to be published. By chance, I heard about the publication of an English version on the 100th anniversary of my mother's birth.

To find pictures for the English edition, I looked through my mother's old photos again, and was confronted with her whole life in them once more.

This time, I noticed that the Chinese and English version of my mother's diploma from Yenching University, as well as her Middle and High School diplomas from McTyeire School for Girls, and my father's diploma from MIT, were all bundled together. They had been recovered from an envelope that had been shut away in a room for thirty years. I have no idea why they put these documents in the old house on Haifang Road, rather than the family home on Wuyi Road. Obviously, it is a good thing that they did, because they have survived to this day. Otherwise, they would certainly have been lost.

In the Chinese edition of this book, there is one photo that does not really attract much attention. After I looked at it, however, I experienced many thoughts and feelings. It was a picture of my father's box of ashes.

In 1961, when the ashes were returned, they were interred in the ashes hall of the Liyi Villa. A few years later it occurred to my mother that since my maternal grandparents' grave was at the Liyi Villa, with empty space on either side, she could dig a small pit and bury my father's ashes there. At last he would be laid to rest.

However, early in 1967, after the start of the Cultural Revolution, revolutionary peasants from the suburbs sent to the graveyard to smash "the four olds" dug up the graves. A week later I heard the news at Tongji University, I rode my bike to Liyi Villa to see the situation for myself. I found gravestones smashed to pieces, all the graves opened, and burial clothes scattered everywhere. There were no bodies or bones to be seen. I checked my maternal grandparents' graves. The gravestones were embedded in a wall behind them, and could not be smashed. However, they had been completely vandalized. The grave covers had been flung to one side, and there was no trace of the two copper coffins. Even the hole containing my father's box of ashes did not escape. The earth had been scooped out and it was totally empty.

That image has stayed with me my whole life. Since moving to America, I have had nightmares about it many times. I have always wondered if the incident lay behind my mother's determination not to be cremated, and to donate her remains to medical research.

When going through the old photos, I also found the final family photo that had my father in it. It was probably taken in 1956 or 1957, when my elder sister came back to visit for the winter holiday. The look in his eyes seemed to have an extra layer of anxiety. It was very rare for our family to go to the photographer's to have a family photo taken. The previous family photo, included in this book, had been taken roughly ten years earlier. I'm not sure whether a premonition of coming misfortune caused my father to hurriedly take us for that family photo. Whatever the circumstances, this photo lacked the joy of the one taken ten years before. It always looks rushed and uneasy when I look at it.

In addition, I also found a photo of Danyan and my mother taken the first time they met. At the time it was just an ordinary photo, taken at a meal the three guests had with my mother, mentioned by Danyan in her book. Looking back, that lunch was actually the beginning of this book about my mother. Sometimes a photo can be magical, fighting the passage of time, preserving those moments that have already been lost in the past. My mother passed away many years ago. My family are spread all over the world, and very few of the younger generation can read Chinese books. My mother's story has been retold many times, becoming almost legendary. Now at last the family can sit peacefully and learn about the many years of her life that she spent in Shanghai, and her history after her relatives and friends had all gone. They can hear my mother's own voice.

At my mother's funeral, Danyan said that through her writing she wanted to make my mother live on in the pages of her book, and today it seems that my mother is truly with us still at all times. Now, with the publication of this long-overdue English edition, she will also be able to tell her story to many more people.

Woo Zhongzheng
Torrance, CA, USA
August 2009

About the Translator
Mavis Gock Yen

*M*avis Yen (1916–2008), an Australian born writer of Chinese descent, was the perfect choice to write the English translation of this fascinating account of the life of Daisy Kwok, written by Chen Danyan. There are striking similarities between their personal life stories. Also, as Mavis carried out extensive research of Chinese immigration in Australia, she was familiar with Daisy's family background.

Mavis Gock Yen was born on 13 February 1916 in Perth, Western Australia. Her father William Gock Ming was part of that massive influx of Chinese men from Guangzhou who came to the Australian goldfields in the 19th century. His older brother was part owner of a successful produce business Wing Hing & Co. in Perth. In 1901 William was summoned to Perth to take over his share of the business. William ran the business successfully and married a local woman, Mabel Jenkins.

The family, with Mavis, her brother and two sisters, moved to Shanghai in 1925, taking up residence in a new house in the International Settlement. Unfortunately, tragedy was to strike shortly after they arrived when Mavis' mother contracted small pox, leading to complications from which she died in 1926. William later remarried and his new wife gave birth to three more children.

Mavis studied at the Public School for Girls in the International Settlement, until she passed the London Matriculation exams in 1933. After living in Sydney Australia for a short time, Mavis worked in a number of offices in Shanghai before the Women's League of Health offered her a position as a health and beauty teacher. She then moved to Hong Kong where she worked in a gymnasium and performed paid office work.

The Japanese occupation of most of South East Asia during World War II forced Mavis to return to Sydney where her brothers and sisters had settled. However in 1946 she again moved back to Shanghai and commenced work with the Chinese Industrial Cooperative Movement where she met her future husband Jeffrey.

When the People's Republic of China was declared in 1949, Mavis and Jeffrey moved to Beijing where Jeffrey worked for the government and Mavis became one of the first English language radio broadcasters on Radio Peking. They got married and had one daughter who was born in 1954.

Mavis became a journalist at Xinhua News Agency, where she polished English articles translated from Chinese and later took up teaching English. The Institute where Mavis worked was occupied by the army in 1968 at the height of the Cultural Revolution. Along with a dozen or so other teachers, Mavis was placed under house arrest within the Institute, interrogated and her life history openly examined and criticized.

Six months later the Institute was moved to the town of Mingkang in Henan Province in central China for the purposes of "re-education." At first the teachers and students made mud bricks, dug ditches, worked on road construction, or swept the streets. Later they moved to farm work where they had to carry the night soil to the fields and mix it with earth and plough the soil with a harrow drawn by buffalo.

In 1971 new developments took place as China began to open up to the outside world, although little of this news filtered through to the countryside. To her surprise, Mavis was returned to Beijing with the students before the harvest was completed. The rest of the institute followed a few months later and from then on her life gradually returned to normal.

Mavis was permitted to leave China in October 1975. This was the first opportunity for many years to meet up again with family members, although they had always kept in touch. She returned to China again in October 1977 with the aim of bringing her daughter back which she did in 1981. Jeffrey chose to remain in China and died there in 2004.

In Australia Mavis experienced what may have been one of the happiest periods of her life. At the age of 65 she settled in Canberra and enrolled at the Australian National University (ANU) as a mature student. After successfully completing her studies, she started writing. She submitted articles and short stories, many of them about China, and had some of them published in newspapers and magazines. She also took an interest in the history of Chinese immigrant families in Australia over the previous 150 years. She interviewed many elderly descendents of these families and wrote a comprehensive history of the Chinese immigrant experience.

In her later life she moved to Sydney to be close to her daughter. It was while living in Sydney that Mavis found Chen Danyan's original Chinese edition of Daisy Kwok's life story, which inspired her to write an English translation. Mavis Yen died peacefully in 2008 at the age of 92 without seeing this book published. However, her commitment to telling the story of 20th century China through the lives of ordinary people caught up in extraordinary events lives on.

Richard Horsburgh
Sydney, Australia
April 2009